ACE YOUR SCIENC

ACE YOUR CHEMISTRY SCIENCE PROJECT

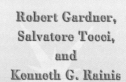

Robert Gardner,
Salvatore Tocci,
and
Kenneth G. Rainis

GREAT SCIENCE FAIR IDEAS

Enslow Publishers, Inc.
40 Industrial Road
Box 398
Berkeley Heights, NJ 07922
USA

http://www.enslow.com

Copyright © 2010 by Robert Gardner, Salvatore Tocci, and Kenneth G. Rainis

All rights reserved.

No part of this book may be reproduced by any means
without the written permission of the publisher.

Library of Congress Cataloging-in-Publication Data

Gardner, Robert, 1929–
    Ace your chemistry science project : great science fair ideas / Robert Gardner, Salvatore
        Tocci, and Kenneth G. Rainis.
        p. cm. — (Ace your science project)
    Includes bibliographical references and index.
    Summary: "Presents several science projects and science project ideas about chemistry"
        —Provided by publisher.
    ISBN-13: 978-0-7660-3227-9
    ISBN-10: 0-7660-3227-2
    1. Chemistry—Experiments—Juvenile literature. 2. Science projects—Juvenile literature.
        I. Tocci, Salvatore. II. Rainis, Kenneth G. III. Title.
    QD38.G344 2010
    540.78—dc22
                             2008030800

Printed in the United States of America
052010 Lake Book Manufacturing, Inc., Melrose Park, IL
10 9 8 7 6 5 4 3 2

To Our Readers: We have done our best to make sure all Internet Addresses in this book were active and appropriate when we went to press. However, the author and the publisher have no control over and assume no liability for the material available on those Internet sites or on other Web sites they may link to. Any comments or suggestions can be sent by e-mail to comments@enslow.com or to the address on the back cover.

♻ Enslow Publishers, Inc., is committed to printing our books on recycled paper. The paper in every book contains 10% to 30% post-consumer waste (PCW). The cover board on the outside of each book contains 100% PCW. Our goal is to do our part to help young people and the environment too!

The experiments in this book are a collection of the authors' best experiments, which were previously published by Enslow Publishers, Inc. in *Crime-Solving Science Projects: Forensic Science Experiments, Science Fair Success in the Hardware Store, Science Fair Success Using Household Products, Science Project Ideas About Air, Science Projects About Kitchen Chemistry,* and *Science Projects About Solids, Liquids, and Gases.*

Illustration Credits: Stephen F. Delisle, Figures 1, 2, 3, 4, 5, 13, 15, 16, 17, 21, 22, 25, 26; Jacob Katari, Figures 6, 7, 8, 9, 10, 11, 12; and Enslow Publishers, Inc., Figures 14, 18, 19, 20, 23, 24.

Cover Photos: © iStockphoto.com/Katya Monakhova (girl); Shutterstock (objects).

CONTENTS

Introduction 5
Science Fair Projects 5
The Scientific Method 6
Science Fairs 8
Safety First 8

CHAPTER 1

Chemical Properties 11

⊙1.1 How Does Bleach Affect Stains? 13
 1.2 How Does Vinegar Affect Galvanized Nails? 15
 1.3 How Thick Is the Galvanized Layer on Metal? 18
 1.4 What Is the Densest Object You Can Find? 24

CHAPTER 2

Acids and Bases 27

⊙2.1 How Do Acids and Bases Affect an Indicator? 29
⊙2.2 Is Grape Juice a Natural Indicator? 32
 2.3 What Happens When an Acid and a Base Mix? 34
 2.4 Using Titration to Determine Acid Concentration 36
⊙2.5 Building a Current Detector to Test Acids and Bases 39
⊙2.6 Making a Battery Pole Indicator Using a Potato 43

CHAPTER 3

Temperature, Volume, and Pressure 45

 3.1 What Is the Temperature of Air in Different Places? 46
 3.2 Air and Pressure: A Bouncing Coin 47
 3.3 How Does Water Depth Affect Pressure? 48
⊙3.4 A Barometer in Water and Air 53
 3.5 Using Air Pressure to Make a Chemist's Pipette and More! ... 55
 3.6 An Egg, a Bottle, and Air Pressure 60

CHAPTER 4

Conductivity and the Effects of Temperature on Matter 63

⊙4.1 Testing Solids and Gases for Electrical Conductivity 64
 4.2 Testing Solids for Thermal (Heat) Conductivity 68

⊙ *Indicates experiments that offer ideas for science fair projects.*

◐4.3 Testing Liquids and Gases for Thermal Conductivity 71
◐4.4 How Does Temperature Affect Gases and Liquids? 75
◐4.5 How Does Temperature Affect Solids? 79
◐4.6 Water's Strange Behavior 82
◐4.7 What Is Convection? 85

CHAPTER 5

Practical Applications of Chemistry   89

◐5.1 Analyzing Aspirin 91
 5.2 Analyzing Aspirin Substitutes 94
 5.3 Using Distillation to Make Pure Water 99
◐5.4 Can Fat Become Soap? 104
◐5.5 Using a Chemical Test to Identify Blood 106

Further Reading and Internet Addresses 109
Index 110

◐ *Indicates experiments that offer ideas for science fair projects.*

INTRODUCTION

When you hear the word *science*, do you think of a person in a white lab coat surrounded by beakers of bubbling liquids, specialized lab equipment, and computers? What exactly is science? Maybe you think science is only a subject you learn in school. Science is much more than this.

Science is the study of the things that are all around you, every day. No matter where you are or what you are doing, scientific principles are at work. You don't need special materials or equipment, or even a white lab coat, to be a scientist. Materials commonly found in your home, at school, or at a local store will allow you to become a scientist and pursue an area of interest. By making careful observations and asking questions about how things work, you can begin to design experiments to investigate a variety of questions. You can do science. You probably already have but just didn't know it!

Perhaps you are reading this book because you are looking for an idea for a science fair project for school, or maybe you are just hoping to find something fun to do on a rainy day. This book will provide an opportunity to conduct experiments and collect data to learn more about chemistry. By doing some of the experiments in this book, you will gain a better understanding of chemistry and have fun along the way!

SCIENCE FAIR PROJECTS

Many of the experiments in this book may be appropriate for science fair projects. Experiments marked with an asterisk (⊙) include a section called Science Fair Project Ideas. The ideas in this section will provide suggestions to help you develop your own original science fair project. However, judges at such fairs do not reward projects or experiments that are simply copied from a book. For example, a model of an atom, commonly found at these fairs, would probably not impress judges unless it was done in a novel way. On the other hand, a carefully performed experiment to find out how temperature affects the solubility of different substances would be likely to receive careful consideration.

THE SCIENTIFIC METHOD

All scientists look at the world and try to understand how things work. They make careful observations and conduct research about a question. Different areas of science use different approaches. Depending on the phenomenon being investigated, one method is likely to be more appropriate than another. Three different objectives such as designing a new medication for heart disease, studying the spread of an invasive plant species such as purple loosestrife, and finding evidence of whether there was once water on Mars, require three very different methods.

Despite the differences, however, all scientists use a similar general approach to do experiments. It is called the scientific method. In most experiments, some or all of the following steps are used: making an observation, formulating a question, making a hypothesis (an answer to the question) and prediction (an if-then statement), designing and conducting an experiment, analyzing results and drawing conclusions, and accepting or rejecting the hypothesis. Scientists then share their findings with others by writing articles that are published in journals. After—and only after—a hypothesis has repeatedly been supported by experiments can it be considered a theory.

You might be wondering how to get an experiment started. When you observe something in the world, you may become curious and think of a question. Your question can be answered by a well-designed investigation. Your question may also arise from an earlier experiment or from background reading. Once you have a question, you should make a hypothesis. Your hypothesis is a possible answer to the question (what you think will happen). Once you have a hypothesis, it is time to design an experiment.

In most cases, it is appropriate to do a controlled experiment. This means there are two groups treated exactly the same except for the single factor that you are testing. That factor is often called a variable.

For example, if you want to investigate whether temperature affects the solubility of sugar in water, you would use two groups. One group is called the control group, and the other is called the experimental group. The two groups should be treated exactly the same: the same type of container should be used in each, the containers should contain the same volume of water, the water should be stirred the same number of times, and so forth. The control group will be the beaker kept in a pan maintained at room temperature while the experimental group will be the beaker kept in a pan maintained at a higher temperature. The variable is temperature—it is the thing that changes, and it is the only difference between the two groups.

During the experiment, you will collect data. In this example, you will measure the amount of sugar (in grams) that dissolves in the water in each beaker. By comparing the data collected from the control group with the data collected from the experimental group, you will draw conclusions. Since the two groups are treated exactly alike except for temperature, an increased number of grams dissolving in the beaker of water maintained at a higher temperature would allow you to conclude with confidence that increased solubility is a result of the one thing that was different: higher temperature.

Two other terms that are often used in scientific experiments are *dependent* and *independent* variables. The dependent variable here is the amount of sugar that dissolves, because solubility depends upon temperature. Temperature is the independent variable. It is the one the experimenter intentionally changes. After the data is collected, it is analyzed to see whether the hypothesis was supported or rejected. Often, the results of one experiment will lead you to a related question, or they may send you off in a different direction. Whatever the results, there is something to be learned from all scientific experiments.

SCIENCE FAIRS

Science fair judges tend to reward creative thought and imagination. It helps if you are really interested in your project. Take the time to choose a topic that really appeals to you. Consider, too, your own ability and the cost of materials. Don't pursue a project that you can't afford.

If you decide to use a project found in this book for a science fair, you will need to find ways to modify or extend it. This should not be difficult because you will probably find that as you do these projects new ideas for experiments will come to mind. These new experiments could make excellent science fair projects, particularly because they spring from your own mind and are interesting to you.

If you decide to enter a science fair and have never done so before, you should read some of the books listed in the Further Reading section. The books that deal specifically with science fairs will provide plenty of helpful hints and lots of useful information that will enable you to avoid the pitfalls that sometimes plague first-time entrants. You will learn how to prepare appealing reports that include charts and graphs, how to set up and display your work, how to present your project, and how to relate to judges and visitors.

SAFETY FIRST

As with many activities, safety is important in science, and certain rules apply when conducting experiments. Some of the rules below may seem obvious to you, but each is important to follow.

1. Have **an adult** help you whenever the experiment advises.

2. Wear eye protection and closed-toe shoes (rather than sandals), and tie back long hair.

3. Do not eat or drink while doing experiments and never taste substances being used.

4. Avoid touching chemicals.

5. Keep flammable substances away from fire.

6. When doing these experiments, use only nonmercury thermometers, such as those filled with alcohol. The liquid in some thermometers is mercury. It is dangerous to breathe mercury vapor. If you have mercury thermometers, **ask an adult** to take them to a local mercury thermometer exchange location.

7. Do only those experiments that are described in the book or those that have been approved by **an adult**.

8. Never engage in horseplay or play practical jokes.

9. Before beginning, read through the entire experimental procedure to make sure you understand all instructions. Clear extra items from your work space.

10. At the end of every activity, clean all materials used and put them away. Wash your hands thoroughly with soap and water.

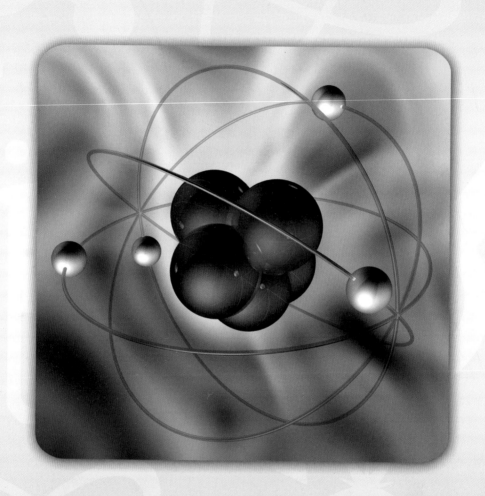

Chapter 1

Chemical Properties

CHEMISTRY IS THE STUDY OF MATTER AND ITS PROPERTIES. Matter is anything that has mass and takes up space. This book is matter, your body is matter, and the air around you is matter.

Matter is made up of very tiny particles called atoms. In turn, atoms are made up of even tinier particles called protons, neutrons, and electrons. Protons carry a positive charge, neutrons are neutral, and electrons carry a negative charge. Protons and neutrons are found in the nucleus at the center of the atom. Electrons move around the nucleus very rapidly, somewhat like the planets orbiting the sun. But unlike the planets, electrons sometimes leave their orbits to join another atom.

Whenever a chemical substance loses electrons, it is said to be oxidized. *Oxidation* is the loss of electrons by a chemical substance. The substance that gains the electrons is said to be reduced. *Reduction* is the gain of electrons by a chemical substance. Oxidation and reduction go hand-in-hand; you cannot have one without the other. Taken together, a reduction reaction and an oxidation reaction are jointly referred to as a redox reaction.

Redox reactions occur not only in chemistry labs but also in many other places, including in and around your home. For example, a redox reaction causes rust to form on a car or an iron gate. Rust forms when iron becomes oxidized by the oxygen in the air. As iron is oxidized, it loses electrons to oxygen atoms in the atmosphere. The iron and oxygen react to form a compound called iron oxide, which is commonly known as rust. Other metals can also corrode as a result of a redox reaction, although we do not call the resulting product rust. Obviously, inhibiting the redox reaction prevents the formation of rust. To stop rust from forming, metals can be painted or covered with a wax that serves as a barrier between the metal and the oxygen. The barrier prevents the transfer of electrons between them.

You are probably familiar with batteries because you have used them in a flashlight, calculator, or radio. You may already know that batteries use chemical reactions to produce electrical currents. But did you know that batteries operate as a result of one chemical substance losing electrons that another chemical substance gains?

Let's learn more about redox reactions.

Materials:

- an adult
- scissors
- piece of white cotton fabric
- crayon
- lipstick
- tomato juice
- 2 large glass jars of the same size
- marking pen
- liquid bleaches with and without chlorine
- measuring cup
- clock or watch
- pair of rubber kitchen gloves
- water

Liquid bleach is a cleaning product you probably have at home. Bleaching is a chemical reaction that removes the color from a substance. When used for washing clothes, bleaches preserve whiteness and remove stains. Care must be taken when using bleaches because they contain chemicals that can damage delicate fabrics such as silk. They can also damage sensitive skin. Repeated use of bleaches may cause cotton fabrics to turn yellow.

One way to avoid these problems is to use bleach that does not contain chlorine. In this experiment, you can compare bleaches with and without chlorine to see how well they remove stains from fabrics. Conduct this experiment outside or in a place with good ventilation so that you do not inhale the fumes from the bleach.

Cut a piece of white cotton fabric into two equal-sized pieces. Stain both pieces with crayon, lipstick, and tomato juice. Try to make the stains—in terms of size and intensity of color—the same on both pieces of fabric. (Plan ways to do this. Why is this important?)

Label one large glass jar as A and another as B. (Why must the jars be the same size?) Place a piece of stained fabric in each of the two jars. **Put on the rubber gloves** to protect your skin. **Under adult supervision,** cover the fabric in jar A with bleach that contains chlorine. Cover the fabric in jar B with bleach lacking chlorine. Be sure that you add the same volume of bleach to each jar. What should be the only independent variable in this experiment?

Allow the fabrics to soak for 30 minutes. Wearing the rubber kitchen gloves, pour the bleaches down a sink. Rinse the fabrics in running water for several minutes. Remove them from the jars and examine both fabrics. Was one bleach more effective in getting out stains? Will the less effective bleach work as well as the other if the fabric soaks in it for a longer time?

 ## Science Fair Project Idea

Bleaches work by causing a redox reaction. In both cases, the bleaching action works by changing a colored substance (stain) into a colorless substance. In other words, the substance that caused the stain is still in the fabric. But this substance is no longer visible because the bleach caused it to become colorless.

Carry out a project that investigates how bleaches work in removing stains. You will first need to learn more about redox reactions. Ask a chemistry teacher for guidance. Compare the two types of bleaches in terms of their efficiency, rate of action, and how long they retain their bleaching ability. You can also investigate what water temperatures and water softness produce the best results.

1.2 How Does Vinegar Affect Galvanized Nails?

Materials:

- an adult
- vinegar
- galvanized and nongalvanized nails that are small enough to fit into an empty plastic pill container
- empty plastic pill container
- candle
- matches
- oven mitt
- tongs

In Experiment 1.1, you used the redox reactions of bleaches to remove stains. In some cases, redox reactions are not so helpful. Some substances are made in a special way to prevent oxidation or reduction. For example, some metals are coated with paint or wax. Others are coated with a thin layer of another metal in a process known as *galvanization*. The word *galvanization* comes from the name Luigi Galvani, an Italian scientist who studied electricity during the 1700s. In fact, batteries are also known as galvanic cells in his honor.

In this experiment, you will be working with galvanized nails. A thin layer of zinc metal covers the iron nail. Zinc is a more active metal than iron. *Active* means it will give up its electrons more readily to oxygen in the air. As a result, the zinc rusts before the iron can. In effect, the zinc is sacrificed to save the iron. In addition, the compound that forms when zinc and oxygen react serves as a protective barrier for the iron underneath. Here is a simple experiment using galvanized nails to prove that zinc is a more active metal than iron. You will collect one of the products made when a metal reacts with an acid.

Place several galvanized nails in an empty plastic pill container. Pour vinegar into the container until it is three-quarters full. Place the cap on the container and invert it. Allow the nails to soak in the vinegar overnight. Look for tiny gas bubbles that form in the vinegar.

The next day, **ask an adult** to light a candle. Over a sink, remove the cap while keeping the pill container inverted. Allow the nails and vinegar to drain into the sink. Using tongs and wearing an oven mitt, quickly bring the mouth of the container up to the candle flame, as shown in Figure 1. Listen to what happens. Repeat the process, this time using nails that are not galvanized.

The reaction between the acid in the vinegar and the metal produces hydrogen gas. These are the tiny bubbles that you should have seen forming in the vinegar as the nails soaked. The more violent the reaction, the more hydrogen gas produced. The more hydrogen gas produced, the more the metal has reacted with the acid in the vinegar.

When a flame or spark is introduced, hydrogen gas reacts violently with oxygen gas in the air to produce water. That's why you probably heard a pop when you moved the pill container close to the flame.

Which metal reacted more with the acid: the zinc that coats a galvanized nail or the iron of a nongalvanized nail? By the way, can you think of a reason why you had to keep the pill container inverted while you brought it to the flame?

ALLOYS

Actually, the nongalvanized nails that you used in this experiment are not made entirely of iron. If they were, they would be too soft to hammer. Rather, they are made of steel, which is an alloy. An *alloy* is a mixture of two or more metals. Nonmetals can also be added to an alloy. For example, the steel used for nails is a 99.8 percent metal alloy (mostly iron) and less than 0.2 percent carbon, which is a nonmetal. That small percentage of carbon gives the alloy the properties needed so that nails can be hammered. Tools such as hammers and screwdrivers are made from

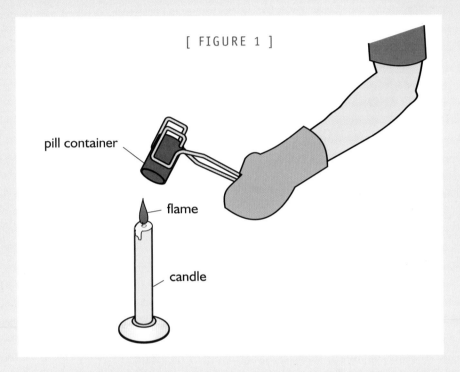

[FIGURE 1]

pill container

flame

candle

You should hear a small pop when you hold the empty pill container over the flame. The more galvanized nails you soak in vinegar, the bigger the pop.

high-carbon steel. This steel contains between 0.6 percent and 1.5 percent carbon. The higher the carbon content, the tougher and harder the metal.

Steel is not the only alloy that has been put to practical use. Another is brass, an alloy used to make screws and various hardware items such as hinges and doorknobs. Brass contains the metals copper, zinc, tin, lead, and manganese. Still another alloy is based on the metal titanium. Titanium alloys are quite strong. Over 10,000 pounds of titanium alloys are used to build each engine in a 747 jet airplane. In contrast, the amount of zinc used to produce a galvanized layer is quite small.

Materials:

- an adult
- centimeter ruler
- kitchen scale
- vinegar
- piece of galvanized metal
- metal shears
- glass or plastic container large enough to hold metal upright
- water
- paper towels

The layer of zinc metal that is used to galvanize an object such as a nail is very thin. You can actually determine the thickness of the zinc layer based on the density of the metal. *Density* is the ratio of mass to volume. *Mass* is simply how much "stuff" there is. *Volume* is the amount of space the "stuff" occupies. Density is a measure of how tightly matter is packed. Which of the objects shown in Figure 2 is more dense?

Density is usually expressed in units of grams per milliliter, or g/ml. Another way of expressing density is in units of grams per cubic centimeter, or g/cm^3. The density of zinc is 7.14 g/cm^3. With the use of this value, you can determine the thickness of the zinc layer on a galvanized object. In this experiment, you may want to have your science teacher check the calculations that are required in the results.

If you cannot find any galvanized metal at home, ask at a hardware store or a junkyard for a scrap piece. **Ask an adult** to use metal shears to cut the piece of metal into the shape of a rectangle so that it can fit upright into a glass or plastic container. Use a kitchen scale to determine the mass of the metal. Record the mass of the metal in grams. If your kitchen scale is not calibrated in grams, then use the following conversion:

$$1 \text{ ounce} = 28 \text{ grams}$$

[FIGURE 2]

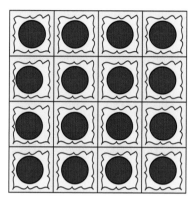

candy box A

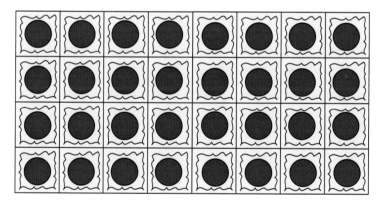

candy box B

Because density is a ratio, you must consider both the mass and the volume of an object. The candy box on the bottom has twice the volume of the other but also contains twice as many candies. As a result, both these boxes have the same mass-to-volume ratio. Thus both candy boxes have the same density.

Measure the length and width of the metal in centimeters (cm). Place the metal in the container and cover it with vinegar. Allow the metal to remain in the vinegar until all the zinc that forms the coating has reacted with the acid. You can tell that the reaction is complete when no more hydrogen gas bubbles form. To be sure that all the zinc has reacted, replace the vinegar with a fresh supply. If no gas bubbles form after the vinegar has been replenished, then all the zinc has reacted.

Pour the used vinegar down a drain. Remove the metal, rinse it thoroughly with running water, and dry it with paper towels. Reweigh the metal. The metal should weigh less because the zinc has been removed. Calculate the mass of the zinc used to coat the metal. Do this by subtracting the mass of the metal after it was placed in the vinegar from the mass of the metal before it was placed in the vinegar.

Calculate the area of the metal rectangle by multiplying the length by the width. Because the zinc metal coats both sides, the area covered by the zinc is twice the area of the galvanized metal you measured. Express your answer in square centimeters (cm^2).

Next, calculate the volume of zinc on the metal. To do this, multiply the mass of the zinc by the inverse of the density of the zinc. The mass units (g) will cancel, leaving the volume unit (cm^3).

$$\cancel{g} \text{ zinc} \times \frac{1 \text{ cm}^3}{7.14 \cancel{g}} = cm^3 \text{ (volume covered by zinc)}$$

Next, divide the volume of zinc on the metal (cm^3) by the area of the metal rectangle (cm^2).

$$\frac{\text{volume zinc } (cm^3)}{\text{area zinc } (cm^2)} = \text{thickness of zinc (cm)}$$

For an added challenge, calculate the thickness of the zinc coating in terms of the number of zinc atoms that form the coat. The radius of a zinc atom is 2.66×10^{-8} cm.

METRIC SYSTEM

In this experiment, you recorded your measurements and performed your calculation using centimeters (cm) and grams (g). These units are part of the metric system. Scientists use the metric system, a system based on tens. As a result, conversions between units are easy to perform, unlike the system used in the United States. Just consider what you have to do when converting gallons to fluid ounces. You first have to multiply the number of gallons by 4 to convert to quarts. Then you have to multiply this value by 32 to convert to fluid ounces. Thus, 1.2 gallons = 4.8 quarts = 153.6 fluid ounces.

Now consider what you do when converting volume units in the metric system. To convert liters to centiliters, you multiply by 100 or move the decimal point two places to the right. To convert centiliters to milliliters, you multiply by 10 or move the decimal point one place to the right. Thus, 1.2 liters = 120 centiliters = 1,200 milliliters. You can see that you do not need a calculator to perform conversions in the metric system once you recognize what the prefixes mean. Table 1 lists the common prefixes used in the metric system. How many grams are equal to 75.68 milligrams?

TABLE 1
Metric Prefixes

Prefix	Units	Symbol	Meaning
giga–	10^9	G	billion
mega–	10^6	M	million
kilo–	10^3	k	thousand
deci–	10^{-1}	d	tenth
centi–	10^{-2}	c	hundredth
milli–	10^{-3}	m	thousandth
micro–	10^{-6}	μ	millionth
nano–	10^{-9}	n	billionth

Now you recognize the advantage of the metric system: the ease of converting between units. Keep in mind that the metric system is not more accurate than any other system of measurements, including the one used in the United States. You can measure the length of your room just as accurately in yards as you can in meters. However, converting the value in yards to inches is more involved mathematically than converting the value in meters to centimeters.

Chemists and other scientists throughout the world use the metric system for their measurements in the laboratory. In 1960, the scientific community adopted a subset of the metric system to use as the standard scientific system of measurement units. This is the *Le Système International d'Unités*, or SI for short. The SI system includes seven base units that are listed in Table 2. Any SI unit can be modified with prefixes to match the scale of the object being measured. While meters may be suitable to measure a person's height, micrometers (10^{-6} m) are more appropriate for measuring the size of cells.

TABLE 2
SI Base Units

Quantity	Unit	Symbol
length	meter	m
mass	kilogram	kg
time	second	s
temperature	kelvin	K
amount	mole	mol
electric current	ampere	A
luminous intensity	candela	cd

The seven SI base units cannot measure every observable property. Thus, derived units are created by either multiplying or dividing the seven base units in various ways. For example, in the previous experiment, the volume of zinc on the metal was expressed in cm^3 (cm × cm × cm). The area covered by the zinc was expressed in cm^2 (cm × cm). If you had to measure the speed of an object, you would divide the distance traveled, using the base unit meter (m), by the time it took, using the base unit second (s). Thus, speed could be expressed as m/s, which can then be converted to km/hour.

Materials:
- assortment of nails and screws
- metric scale or balance
- water
- metric measuring cup (the smaller the better)

You probably use the metric system when you carry out a science experiment in school. For example, you may have measured the volume of a liquid in milliliters or the mass of an object in grams. But chances are that your science classroom is the only place you have used the metric system. The following experiment will give you an opportunity to practice using the metric system at home. It will also allow you to better understand density and to measure volume using water displacement.

You will determine which is the densest nail or screw that you can find.

Obtain an assortment of different types of nails and screws, including those made of both galvanized and nongalvanized metals and brass. Check with an employee at a hardware store if you are not sure what metals are present in the different nails and screws that you find.

Earlier in this chapter, you read that density is usually expressed in the units g/ml. These are the units you will use to calculate the density of each type of nail and screw. But first you must learn how to measure volumes using the water displacement method. Simply pour some water into a measuring cup marked in milliliters (ml). Record the volume of water you added. You will find it convenient to add the water up to one of the lines marked on the cup, for example the 100 ml mark. Next drop in one nail or screw and see how much the volume increases. This represents the volume occupied by that object.

One nail or screw most likely did not cause a noticeable increase in the volume, especially if you used a large measuring cup. In that case, drop in ten, twenty, or as many identical nails or screws as necessary until you can measure an increase in volume. Make sure that all the

[FIGURE 3]

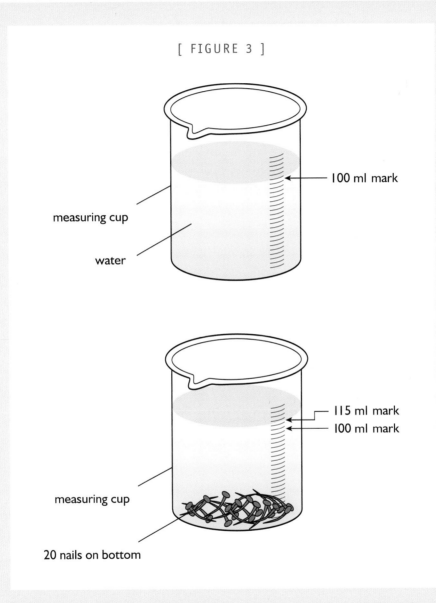

100 ml mark

measuring cup

water

115 ml mark
100 ml mark

measuring cup

20 nails on bottom

The 20 nails that were added to this measuring cup caused the volume to increase from 100 ml to 115 ml. Thus 20 nails were responsible for an increase in volume of 15 ml. Each nail therefore occupies a volume of 15 ml/20 nails = 0.75 ml/nail.

CHEMICAL PROPERTIES **25**

objects you drop in are made of the same metal or alloy and are the same size. To determine the volume of just one of the objects, divide the volume increase by the number of objects you placed in the measuring cup. For example, the volume occupied by one nail in Figure 3 is 0.75 ml.

Once you know the volume of the object, determine its mass by placing it on a scale. If one nail or screw does not register a noticeable increase in mass, then place ten or twenty of them on the scale. Again be sure to divide the total increase in mass by the number of objects you weighed to get the mass of just one object. Now divide the mass of the object by the volume you obtained earlier to calculate the density of that object. Prepare a table listing the densities of each type of nail and screw you measured.

None of the densities you calculated will even come close to that of osmium, a blue-white metal. With a density of 22.6 g/ml, osmium is the densest substance on Earth. It is so dense that a piece of osmium the size of a football would be too heavy for you to lift. If you can measure the volume of a football, then you should be able to determine how much this sample of osmium would weigh. Simply multiply the volume (ml) of the football by its density (g/ml). Notice that the volume units (ml) cancel, leaving the mass unit (g).

Chapter 2

Acids and Bases

TWO TYPES OF CHEMICALS THAT CHEMISTS WORK WITH ARE ACIDS AND BASES. *Acid* comes from the Latin word *acidus*, meaning "sharp" or "sour." That is how sour-tasting foods and chemicals came to be known as acids. In addition to their sour taste, acids dissolve in water to form solutions that conduct electricity; they contain hydrogen that is released when the acid is added to certain metals such as zinc; they turn blue litmus red; and they neutralize bases: that is, they combine with a base to form a substance that is neither an acid nor a base. Substances that are neither acidic nor basic, such as water, are said to be neutral.

Bases are also called *alkalis*, a word that means "ashes." Long before there were chemists there were ashes, the remains of wood after burning. Ashes have the properties that chemists use to identify alkaline substances, or bases. Bases have a bitter taste and feel slippery like soap. Early American settlers made soap by boiling animal fat with wood ashes that had been washed. Bases, like acids, are conductors of electricity, but they turn red litmus blue, have a bitter taste, and neutralize acids.

Acids and bases conduct electricity because they form charged atoms, called *ions*, when they dissolve in water. Acids form hydrogen ions (H^+) and bases form hydroxide ions (OH^-). This chemical equation should help you understand how acids and bases neutralize one another to form water (HOH, or H_2O):

$$H^+ + OH^- \rightarrow HOH, \text{ or } H_2O$$

Did you know that many acids and bases are found in your home? The experiments in this chapter will demonstrate the properties of acids and bases.

Materials:

- an adult
- lemon juice
- red cabbage
- nonaluminum cooking pot and cover
- stove
- water
- clock
- forceps or tongs
- 2 jars with lids
- refrigerator
- eyedropper
- vinegar
- small glass jars or test tubes
- clear household ammonia
- apple juice, grapefruit juice, and orange juice
- milk
- cleansing powder
- rubbing alcohol
- salt and sugar
- aspirin
- wood ashes
- baking soda and baking powder
- lime from a garden center (to make limewater)
- Kool-Aid crystals
- Tang crystals
- juice from a jar of olives
- juice from a jar of pickles
- ginger ale
- tonic water
- seltzer water
- pen or pencil and paper

Place a drop of lemon juice on your tongue. Do you think lemon juice is an acid or a base? Why?

To test your hypothesis, you might dip pieces of red and blue litmus into the liquid. However, since we are dealing with household chemicals, you can make your own acid-base indicator.

Remove a few leaves from a red cabbage. Break the leaves into small pieces and put them in a nonaluminum cooking pot. Cover the leaves with water and, **under adult supervision,** put the pot on the stove. When the water begins to boil, cover the pan and turn down the heat so that the water boils quietly. After about 20 minutes, remove the pot from the stove and let it cool.

When the pot is cool, use forceps or tongs to remove the cabbage leaves. Pour the water and cabbage juice extracted from the leaves into a jar. Store it in the refrigerator until you are ready to use it.

The color of cabbage juice, like the color of litmus, is affected by acids and bases. The purplish cabbage juice that you have prepared will turn a pinkish red in an acid and green in a base. It is a more sensitive indicator than litmus because in a very weak base—one that forms few hydroxide ions in water—it will have a bluish tint. In a weak acid—one that forms few hydrogen ions—the pinkish red is less intense.

You can use your cabbage juice indicator to test a number of household chemicals to see whether they are acidic, basic, or neutral. To do this, add a few drops of each substance to a small amount of cabbage juice indicator and look at the color. For solid substances, you should add water to make a small amount of solution before adding a drop of the cabbage juice indicator. In addition to lemon juice, you might try vinegar, clear household ammonia, apple juice, grapefruit juice, orange juice, milk, cleansing powder, rubbing alcohol, salt, sugar, aspirin, wood ashes, baking soda, baking powder, limewater, Kool-Aid crystals, Tang crystals, the juice from an olive jar, pickle juice, ginger ale, tonic water, and seltzer water. You can make limewater for testing by obtaining lime from a garden supply store. Stir one teaspoon of the white solid into a small jar of water. Put a lid on the jar and let the mixture settle overnight. Carefully pour the liquid into a second jar, leaving any white solid behind.

Make a chart with three columns. Label one column *acids*, another *bases*, and a third *neutral*. On the basis of the color you saw when cabbage juice was added, place the names of the substances you tested in the proper column.

Science Fair Project Ideas

- Vitamin C, as you may know, is ascorbic acid. Crush a vitamin C tablet into a powder and add some water. Predict the color of the cabbage juice indicator after it is added to the vitamin C solution. Were you right?
- You have seen that cabbage juice is an acid-base indicator. Test a number of other fruits and vegetables to see if you can find other natural acid-base indicators.

Materials:

- lemon juice
- hot tea
- unsweetened red grape juice
- eyedropper
- white vinegar
- small glass jars or test tubes
- clear household ammonia
- water
- apple juice, grapefruit juice, and orange juice
- milk
- cleansing powder
- rubbing alcohol
- salt and sugar
- aspirin
- wood ashes
- baking soda and baking powder
- lime from a garden center (to make limewater)
- Kool-Aid crystals
- Tang crystals
- juice from a jar of olives
- juice from a jar of pickles
- ginger ale
- tonic water
- seltzer water

Add some lemon juice to a cup of hot tea. What evidence do you have that tea is an acid-base indicator? There are many natural acid-base indicators. You have used red cabbage juice; now try unsweetened red grape juice. Add a few drops of the unsweetened grape juice to several milliliters of white vinegar in a small glass jar or test tube. What is the color of the grape juice in an acid? Add a few drops of the grape juice to a few milliliters of ammonia solution. What is the color of the grape juice in a base?

Add a few drops of grape juice to some tap water. What is the color of the grape juice indicator in a neutral solution? Why is cabbage juice a better indicator than grape juice?

Based on the tests you did in the previous experiment, predict the color of unsweetened grape juice in each of the substances you tried before. Then test your predictions experimentally.

 ## Science Fair Project Ideas

- You can use what you have learned about acid-base indicators and neutralization to carry out what will look like magic to your friends and family. To prepare for your show, dilute 20 ml (2/3 oz.) of unsweetened red grape juice with 180 ml (6 oz.) of water to reduce the intensity of the color. Pour the diluted juice into a glass. In a second glass, place a few drops of ammonia solution. When you pour the grape juice into the second glass, it will turn green because ammonia is a base. In a third glass, place more than enough vinegar to neutralize the base. (You will need to practice to get the right amounts of ammonia and vinegar.) When you pour the green liquid into the third glass, it turns back to a red liquid because the excess vinegar makes the liquid acidic again. **Do not put anything with ammonia in it near or in your mouth.**

  Tell your friends and/or family that you can change red liquid to green liquid and then back to red again. Then proceed to use the chemicals you have prepared to carry out your "magic."

- Do some research to add more chemical "magic" until you have a show that you can use to entertain friends, classmates, and students in lower grades.

Materials:

- white vinegar
- measuring teaspoon or graduated cylinder
- small jar or beaker
- red cabbage juice
- eyedropper
- water
- spoon or other stirring device
- clear household ammonia
- baking soda
- pan or sink

One characteristic of acids and bases is their ability to neutralize one another. To see how an acid and a base combine to form a neutral substance, pour about 10 ml (2 teaspoons) of vinegar into a small jar or beaker. Add a few drops of red cabbage juice. Stir the mixture until it has a uniform color. Rinse the eyedropper, then use it to add clear household ammonia drop by drop to the vinegar. Look carefully to see what happens to the color of the solution around the area where the ammonia drops land. Now stir the liquid as you add the drops until you see a distinct color change. What has happened?

Rinse the eyedropper again, then use it to add drops of vinegar to the basic solution. Do this a drop at a time. Notice the effect of one drop on the color of the solution. Look for an intermediate purple color (the color of cabbage juice in neutral water) just before the solution changes from acid to base or base to acid. When you see the indicator turn purple, the solution is neutral.

What happens to the color of the neutral solution if you add a drop or two of vinegar? A drop or two of ammonia?

A drop or two of an acid can turn a neutral solution acidic. But suppose you have something that reacts with the acid. What will happen then? To find out, add some water to a teaspoonful of baking soda in a small jar or beaker. Add a few drops of the indicator to the baking soda. Set the jar or beaker in a pan or in the sink. (You'll soon see why.) Now slowly add vinegar to the solution. Once you reach the neutralization point, is the color change from neutral to acidic sudden or gradual? Try to explain why.

Materials:

- an adult
- 2 pairs of safety goggles
- 2 pairs of rubber gloves
- granulated drain cleaner (contains lye)
- scale that measures in grams (g)
- distilled water
- muriatic acid
- measuring cup graduated in milliliters (mL)
- 2 small plastic squeeze bottles that deliver single drops (Those used for carrying shampoo when traveling can be used.)
- phenolphthalein indicator (borrowed from your science teacher)
- rubbing alcohol
- paper towel
- hammer
- wooden board
- small glass jar
- coffee filter
- tall drinking glass
- dropper

A strong acid can dissolve metals. A strong base can unclog a drain. But if you mix an acid and a base in just the right way, you get a salt solution that cannot melt metals or unclog drains. As you learned in the previous experiment, the acid and base neutralize each other. A reaction in which an acid and a base are neutralized to produce a salt solution is called a *neutralization* reaction. You can carry out a neutralization reaction to determine the concentration of an acid or a base.

Acid Concentration

In this experiment, you can determine the concentration of an acid used to clean pools by neutralizing it with a base that is used to unclog drains. The procedure you will use is called a *titration*. A titration is a procedure in which a solution of known concentration is used to determine the concentration of a second, unknown solution. You will prepare a basic solution with a known concentration. You will then use this solution to determine the concentration of an acid solution that is used to clean pools. This acid, called muriatic acid, is available from hardware stores. You will need **an adult** to prepare the muriatic acid solution that you will use in this experiment.

Put on a pair of safety goggles and a pair of rubber gloves. Ask an adult to do the same. Avoid direct contact with the base and acid solutions that you will use. If you do come in contact with any, immediately wash your skin or clothes with running water.

Ask an adult to prepare a base solution of known concentration by adding 5 g of granulated drain cleaner to a glass jar. Then add 95 ml of distilled water to the jar and stir the solution until all the drain cleaner has dissolved. You now have a 5 percent base solution that you will use to determine the concentration of the acid solution. Fill one of the plastic bottles with the 5 percent base solution and record its mass when filled. Use running water to rinse the glass jar used to make the base solution. Dry the jar for the next step.

Ask an adult to add 20 ml of muriatic acid to 100 ml of distilled water in a glass jar. (**Acid is *always* added to water. Never add water to acid, as the added water may cause the acid to splash toward you.**) Muriatic acid is available in hardware stores and is used to clean certain kinds of swimming pools. The diluted muriatic acid is the solution of unknown concentration. Fill a plastic bottle with the diluted muriatic acid solution and record its mass when filled. Clean and dry the glass jar. Pour about one third of the acid solution in the plastic bottle into the glass jar. Add 3 drops of the phenolphthalein indicator to the acid. Earlier in the chapter, you learned that an indicator changes color depending on whether the solution is an acid or a base. Phenolphthalein is colorless in an acidic solution. In a basic solution, phenolphthalein is pink.

Slowly add the base solution in the plastic bottle drop by drop to the acid in the jar. As you add each drop, continue to swirl the jar to mix the acid and base. Notice that a pink color appears when a drop of base is added but disappears upon swirling. Continue adding the base until one drop causes a pink color that persists for 30 seconds after swirling. At this point, you have reached the end of the titration.

Weigh both plastic bottles. Calculate the amount of acid you used by subtracting the mass of the bottle at the end of the titration from the mass of the bottle when it was full at the start of the experiment. Do the same to calculate the amount of base you added. The concentration of the acid solution is calculated by comparing the ratio of acid and base that were used. For example, if you used 25 g of acid and 25 g of base, their ratio would be 1:1. Because the concentration of the base was 5 percent, then the concentration of the acid would also be 5 percent. However, if you used twice as much base to neutralize the acid, then the ratio of base to acid would be 2:1. Because you used twice as much base to neutralize the acid, the acid would be twice the concentration of the base. In that case, the acid concentration would be 2 × 5 percent, or 10 percent. If you used half as much base to neutralize the acid, then the ratio of base to acid would be 1:2. Because you used half as much base, the acid would be half the concentration of the base. In that case, the acid concentration would be 1/2 × 5 percent, or 2.5 percent.

Under adult supervision, you can use this procedure to determine the concentration of the acid in various household solutions, including vinegar and club soda. Once you know the concentration of an acidic solution, you can use it to determine the concentration of a household solution that is basic, such as ammonia or toilet bowl cleaner. **Never mix ammonia and bleach.**

2.5 Building a Current Detector to Test Acids and Base

Materials:

- enameled copper magnet wire
- magnetic compass
- sandpaper
- ruler
- masking tape
- 3 insulated wires with alligator clips
- 6-volt lantern battery
- 2 large steel paper clips
- plastic vial
- liquids identified as acids or bases using red cabbage juice in Experiment 2.1
- tap water
- distilled water
- salt solution

Another characteristic of acids and bases is their *conductivity*, or ability to conduct electricity. Acids and bases conduct electricity because they form ions in water. For example, vinegar, which is a solution of acetic acid ($C_2H_4O_2$), forms hydrogen ions (H^+) and acetate ions ($C_2H_3O_2^-$) in water. A base such as ammonia solution forms hydroxide ions (OH^-) and ammonium ions (NH_4^+) in water. Because acids and bases form ions in water, their solutions contain charged particles that can move, creating an electric current (a flow of charge).

The acids you have used in this chapter, such as vinegar and lemon juice, are weak acids. Strong acids, such as sulfuric, hydrochloric, and nitric acids, form large numbers of hydrogen ions in water and are more dangerous to work with because they can damage flesh. Weak acids do not form nearly as many ions; consequently, they do not conduct electricity nearly as well as strong acids. Similarly, weak bases, such as ammonia, produce far fewer hydroxide ions than do strong and more dangerous bases, such as sodium hydroxide (NaOH). Nevertheless, weak acids and bases should carry a small current when connected to a battery. Batteries use chemical reactions to produce electric current.

You can build an inexpensive device like the one in Figure 4 to test liquids for conductivity. Make a current detector by wrapping 50 turns of enameled copper magnet wire around a magnetic compass. The enamel serves to insulate the wire. Leave about 15 cm (6 in) of wire at each end of the coil for connecting lead wires to the battery. Use a small piece of sandpaper to remove the insulating enamel from the last 3 cm (1 in) of each end of the coil. The coils, which can be held together with small pieces of masking tape, should be parallel to the compass needle.

To see how the detector works, connect each end of the coil to an insulated wire. Connect one wire to one pole of the battery. Then momentarily touch the other wire to the other pole of the battery. What happens to the compass needle when electricity flows through the coil that surrounds it?

Put two large paper clips on opposite sides of a plastic vial. Use insulated wires with alligator clips to connect one paper clip to a pole of a lantern battery and the other paper clip to a lead of the current detector. Clip the other insulated wire to the current detector. Leave the other end of this wire free.

In Experiment 2.1, you tested various liquids with red cabbage juice. Now you can take those liquids that your indicator revealed to be acids or bases and test them for conductivity. Fill the vial with one of the liquids you believe to be an acid or a base. The paper clips will serve as electrodes, and the liquid will become part of the circuit shown in Figure 4. Touch the free wire to the pole of the battery that is not already connected. What happens to the compass needle? Try other liquids that were acids or bases according to the red cabbage juice indicator. Are they conductors?

[FIGURE 4]

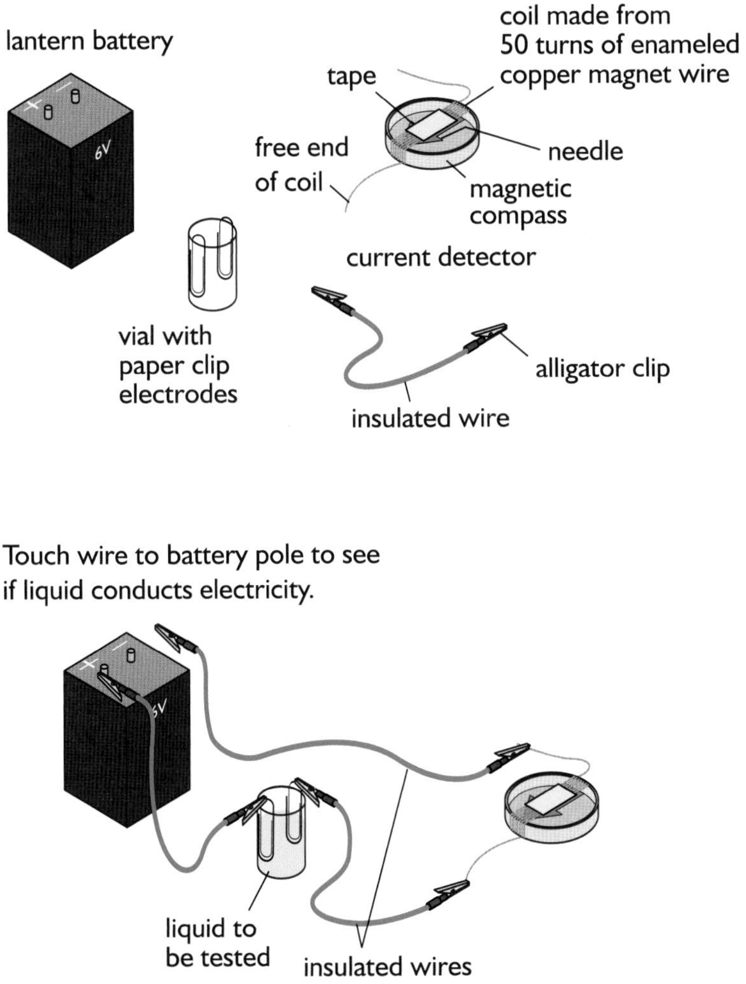

lantern battery

coil made from
50 turns of enameled
copper magnet wire

tape

free end
of coil

needle

magnetic
compass

current detector

vial with
paper clip
electrodes

alligator clip

insulated wire

Touch wire to battery pole to see
if liquid conducts electricity.

liquid to
be tested

insulated wires

**A current detector, battery, wires, and a vial with paper clip
electrodes can be used to test liquid for conductivity.**

Compare the deflection of the compass needle that you find for liquids you believe to be acids or bases with the deflection you obtain with tap water. Does tap water contain any ions? How about distilled water?

Because salt is made up of ions, a salt solution contains many more charged particles than a weak acid or base. To compare the conductivity of a salt solution with weak acids and bases, pour some salt solution into the vial and test for conductivity. How does the deflection of the compass needle compare with the deflection you obtained for a weak acid or a weak base?

 Science Fair Project Idea

Test some other substances to see whether they will conduct electricity. Do you think a sugar solution will conduct electricity? How about cooking oil? Alcohol? Egg white? Test your predictions. Were you correct?

2.6 Making a Battery Pole Indicator Using a Potato

Materials:

- potato
- knife
- 2 insulated wires with alligator clips
- 2 pieces of copper
- 6-volt lantern battery

In the previous experiment, it did not matter to which battery pole the ends of the wire coil were connected, as long as they were connected to opposite poles. However, in experiments where the direction of the current flow is important, one needs to know whether a wire lead is connected to the positive or negative pole of the battery. Usually, the poles are marked with a + or a −, but if they are not, or if the marks have been rubbed off, you can still identify the poles. All you need is a freshly cut potato, two insulated wires with alligator clips, and two pieces of copper. You can use copper nails, short lengths of heavy copper wire, or two copper pennies.

Push the pieces of copper into the freshly cut surface of a potato, as shown in Figure 5. The two pieces of copper will serve as electrodes for the potato, which contains charged particles. Because the flesh of a potato contains charged particles, it can conduct charge just as acids, bases, and salt solutions can. Connect two wires to the copper electrodes and to the poles of a 6-volt lantern battery that are identified as + and −. Wait a few minutes. Around which electrode does a greenish color appear? Is this electrode connected to the positive or negative pole of the battery? (You may be able to see small bubbles of hydrogen being released at the other electrode.) How can a potato be used to identify the pole of a battery?

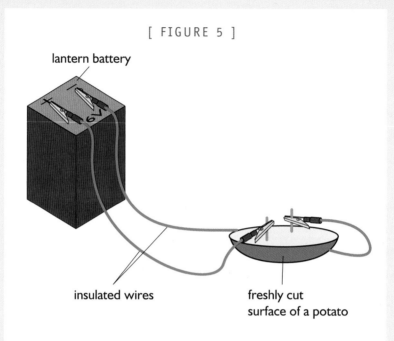

[FIGURE 5]

lantern battery

insulated wires

freshly cut
surface of a potato

A potato and copper electrodes can be used to identify the
poles of a battery.

 Science Fair Project Idea

Do some research to determine why a
greenish color appears around one electrode,
while bubbles of hydrogen form at the other
electrode. Hints: What is the color of many
copper salts when dissolved in water? What
is the metal in the magnet wire?

Chapter 3

Temperature, Volume, and Pressure

TEMPERATURE AND PRESSURE ARE TWO VERY IMPORTANT CONCEPTS TO UNDERSTAND WHEN LEARNING CHEMISTRY. You are affected by both of these every day whether you realize it or not. *Temperature* is a measure of how warm or cold something is. When the air is cold, heat flows from your body to the cold air. You try to reduce heat loss from your body by wearing layers of clothing. When the air is hot, heat flows more slowly from your body. You may even produce heat inside your body faster than it flows out. If the air is warmer than your body, heat will flow from the air into your body. In either case, you will sweat. The evaporation of sweat helps to cool your body.

Pressure is another important concept in chemistry that affects you in your daily life. Pressure is the push (force) that something exerts on the area that it touches. When you stand on a floor, the pressure you exert on the floor is your weight spread over the area of the soles of your feet. Pressure can be measured in newtons per square meter, pounds per square inch, or other units. A barometer can be used to measure air pressure.

3.1 What Is the Temperature of Air in Different Places?

Materials:
- outdoor alcohol thermometer
- building with basement and attic and an outside area
- blacktop area with grassy area nearby

You can measure temperature with a thermometer. On a bright sunny day, take a thermometer outside and measure the temperature of the air in different places. Be sure you leave the thermometer in each place for several minutes. The liquid level in the thermometer should not be changing when you read the thermometer.

Go outside and measure the temperature on the north side of a building such as your house or school. Then measure the temperature on the south side of the same building. How do the temperatures compare? Can you explain any differences?

How does the air temperature over blacktop compare with the air temperature over a grassy area nearby? How does the temperature in a sunny area compare with the temperature in a shady place?

During the same day, measure the temperature on the east and west side of the building. Do this at different times of the same day. How do these temperatures compare? Can you explain any differences?

If it is spring or fall when the building is not being heated or cooled, measure some temperatures inside. How do the air temperatures in the basement, on the ground floor, and in the attic compare? Can you explain any differences in temperature that you find at these various levels?

Measure the temperature near the floor of a room. Then measure the temperature near the ceiling. How do these two temperatures compare? Can you explain any difference in temperature that you find at these different levels in the room?

3.2 Air and Pressure: A Bouncing Coin

Materials:
- basin or pail
- sink
- narrow-necked glass bottle
- water
- coin
- hot and cold tap water

Place a small plastic pail or basin in a large sink. Stand an empty narrow-necked glass bottle upright in the pail or basin. Moisten the mouth of the bottle with a wet finger. Then completely cover the mouth of the bottle with a coin, as shown in Figure 6. Place your hands around the bottle to warm it. Watch and listen closely. You may see and hear the coin lift and fall back onto the mouth of the bottle.

If you can't produce enough heat with your hands, let hot tap water run into the basin or pail and again watch the coin closely. You will see and hear the coin lift and fall back onto the bottle's mouth. Can you explain why the coin does this? Does this experiment provide any evidence that there is a gas in the bottle? What do you think will happen if you repeat the experiment and let cold tap water run into the basin or pail?

As you saw, when air is heated, its pressure increases. The pressure of the warm gas became large enough to lift the coin covering the mouth of the bottle. The force of the air pushing upward on the coin became greater than the weight of the coin and the force of the air pushing it downward. What else happens to a gas when it is heated?

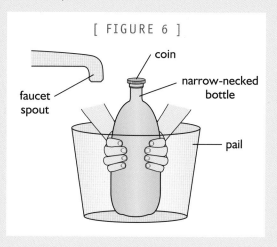

[FIGURE 6]

coin

narrow-necked bottle

faucet spout

pail

First try to use your hands to increase air pressure and make a coin bounce.

Materials:

- an adult
- 2 large cans, such as coffee cans
- hammer
- nail
- masking tape
- water
- sink

Since we live at the bottom of a sea of air, we should expect to experience the weight of that sea. We should find a pressure acting on us, a pressure caused by the tall column of air above us. We certainly feel an increasing pressure when we dive into water. This experiment will show you the pressure in water, which will lead to evidence of air pressure.

To see that water exerts a pressure, find two large cans. **Ask an adult** to help you punch holes in the sides of the cans using a hammer and nail. Be sure the holes are the same size. In one can, punch one hole near the bottom, another near the top, and two in between, as shown in Figure 7a. In the second can, punch five or six holes approximately equal distances apart near the bottom of the can, as shown in Figure 7b. Use masking tape on the outside of the can to cover the holes in both cans.

Fill the two cans with water. Place the can with the holes arranged from top to bottom at the edge of a sink. Turn the can so that water coming out the holes will flow into the sink. Quickly remove the tape from the holes. From which hole does the water project farthest? What does this experiment tell you about pressure as you go deeper in water?

Next, take the can that has six holes punched around it near its bottom. Hold this can over the sink. Quickly remove the tape. How does the projection of water from each hole compare? What can you say about the pressure at the same depth in water? Does it seem to be equal in all directions?

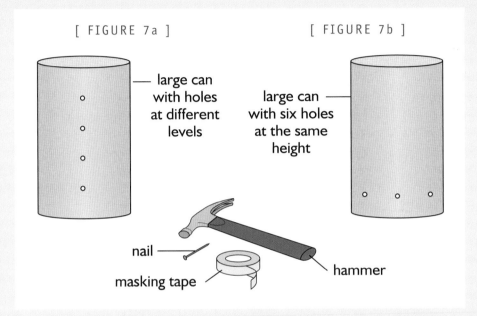

[FIGURE 7a] [FIGURE 7b]

large can with holes at different levels

large can with six holes at the same height

nail

masking tape

hammer

7 a) Holes punched in large cans may be used to show the difference in pressure at different depths of water. b) They can also be used to show that at the same depth, pressure is equal in all directions.

AIR PRESSURE AND BAROMETERS

As discussed in the last experiment, pressure increases as you go deeper in water. But at any one depth, the pressure is equal in all directions. If you have an aneroid barometer, like the one shown in Figure 8a, you can explore the pressure at different depths in the sea of air. An aneroid barometer is not like a mercury barometer. A mercury barometer (see Figure 8b) contains liquid mercury. When the barometer is made, the long tube is filled with mercury. The open end is covered and the tube is turned upside down. The lower end of the tube is placed in a shallow well of mercury. When the cover is removed from the open end, the mercury level falls. Since nothing entered the tube as the mercury fell, the space

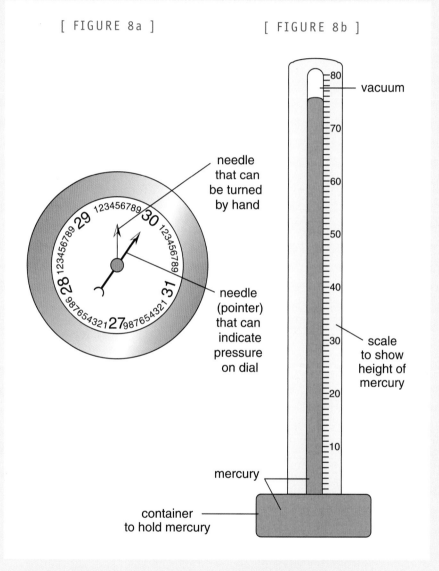

needle
that can
be turned
by hand

needle
(pointer)
that can
indicate
pressure
on dial

vacuum

scale
to show
height of
mercury

mercury

container
to hold mercury

An aneroid barometer (a) and a mercury barometer (b) measure air pressure.

in the tube above the mercury is truly empty. Except for a small amount of mercury vapor, it is a vacuum. If the barometer is at sea level on a normal day, the height of the mercury in the tube will be about 76 cm (30 in) above the mercury level in the well. This column of mercury pushing downward balances the pressure of the air pushing it upward. When air pressure decreases, as it often does when a storm approaches, the height of the mercury column decreases, too.

Barometers can be made using water instead of mercury. But water barometers are not very convenient to read. Because mercury weighs more than 13.5 times as much as an equal volume of water, air pressure will support a column of water more than 10 m (34 ft) tall at sea level.

An aneroid barometer (see Figure 9) has a hole in the back where air can enter. The air pushes against a sealed, thin, round, hollow metal can. Most of the air has been pumped out of the can. The outside of the can is

[FIGURE 9]

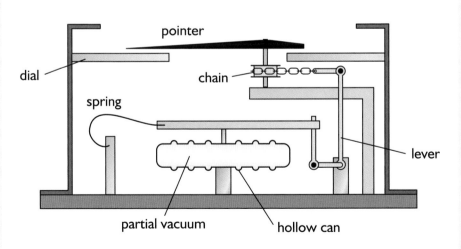

This diagram shows the inside of an aneroid barometer.

attached to a spring. A series of levers connects the spring to a chain that turns a pointer over the dial of the barometer.

When the air pressure increases, the sides of the can are pushed inward. The can then stretches the spring, which pulls on the chain and turns the pointer so that it points toward a larger number on the dial. When air pressure decreases, the sides of the can move outward, the spring is stretched less, and the pointer indicates a smaller number on the dial. Try to explain why the dials on aneroid barometers seldom go below 26 (inches of mercury) or above 32.

3.4 A Barometer in Water and Air

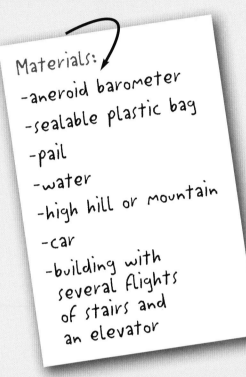

Materials:
- aneroid barometer
- sealable plastic bag
- pail
- water
- high hill or mountain
- car
- building with several flights of stairs and an elevator

Another way to show that pressure increases as you go down into water is to use an aneroid barometer. Place the barometer in a new, sealable plastic bag. Seal the bag. Then watch the dial as you lower the barometer into a pail of water. What happens to the barometer reading as you lower it deeper into the pail?

Now that you've tested the barometer at different depths in water, you can carry it into the sea of air. If we live at the bottom of a sea of air, then we should expect to see the pressure of the air decrease as we go higher into the sea (atmosphere). You can do an experiment to see if this is true. Carry the barometer up a high hill or mountain. Read the barometer dial at the bottom and at the top of the hill or mountain. Does air pressure decrease as you go higher?

Take the barometer with you when you travel by car. Does air pressure increase as you go down a long hill? Does air pressure decrease as you go up a hill?

What happens to air pressure as you go up in an elevator? What happens to the pressure when you go down in an elevator? Can you detect any change in pressure when you climb a flight of stairs? Can you detect any change when you climb several flights of stairs?

Science Fair Project Idea

Your experiments indicate that air pressure, like water pressure, increases as you go deeper into the sea of air. Design an experiment to show that at any point air pressure, like water pressure, is equal in all directions.

Materials:

- an adult
- 2 clear plastic drinking straws
- glass tumbler
- water
- finishing nail and a larger nail
- glass or rigid plastic bottle
- scissors
- paper towel
- sink
- empty coffee can with plastic cover
- empty soup can
- hammer
- masking tape
- petroleum jelly

A DRINKING-STRAW PIPETTE

Chemists use pipettes like the one shown in Figure 10a to transfer liquids from one container to another. You can make a pipette from a drinking straw. Lower a clear plastic drinking straw into a glass of water. Place your index finger or thumb firmly on the top of the straw, as shown in Figure 10b. Now lift the straw out of the water. Notice that the water stays in the straw. What happens when you remove your finger from the top of the straw?

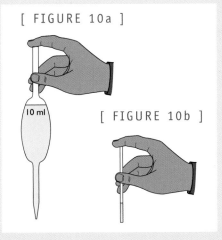

[FIGURE 10a]

10 ml

[FIGURE 10b]

A chemist's pipette (a) or a simple drinking-straw pipette (b) can be used to transfer liquids.

A HOLEY DRINKING STRAW

Use another clear plastic straw to drink water from a glass. Then use a finishing nail to make a hole through the straw about 5 cm (2 in) below its upper end. What happens when you try to drink through the straw now? Can you drink through the straw if you cover the holes with your fingers? What do you think will happen if you try to use this holey straw as a pipette? Try it! Were you right?

THE AMAZING UPSIDE-DOWN BOTTLE OF WATER

Fill a glass or rigid plastic bottle as full as possible with water. Use scissors to cut a piece of paper towel that is slightly larger than the mouth of the bottle. Place the paper on the mouth of the bottle. Turn the bottle upside down over a sink. You will find that the water stays in the bottle, as shown in Figure 11.

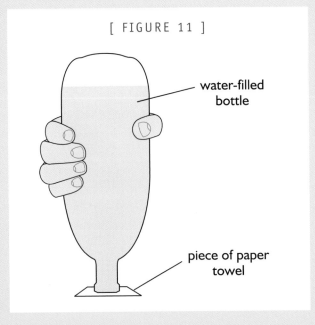

[FIGURE 11]

water-filled bottle

piece of paper towel

An ordinary piece of paper towel can keep water in an upside-down bottle.

TWO WAYS TO PREVENT A CAN FROM LEAKING

Find an empty coffee can with a plastic cover that fits it snugly. Also find an empty soup can. **Ask an adult** to use a hammer and nail to punch a hole in the side of each can near the bottom (see Figure 12). Cover the holes with masking tape. Fill the coffee can with water and place it on the edge of a sink. Use your finger to apply a thin layer of petroleum jelly around the inside of the lip on the plastic cover. The petroleum jelly will act as a seal so that air will not be able to enter the can when you put the cover on the can.

Remove the tape so that water begins to flow from the can and into the sink. Then put the cover on the can. Twist the cover back and forth to make sure the petroleum jelly seals the can and air cannot enter. The water will stop flowing soon after you put the top on the can.

Repeat the experiment with the small can filled with water, but this time use your hand rather than a plastic lid to cover the can. Can you stop the flow of water with your hand?

AIR PRESSURE EFFECTS EXPLAINED

Air pressure can support a column of mercury 76 cm (30 in) high and a column of water 10 m (34 ft) tall, so it is not surprising that it can support a column of water in a bottle as it did in "The Amazing Upside-Down Bottle of Water." When the water in the drinking-straw pipette (in "A Drinking-Straw Pipette") starts to fall out of the straw, it slightly lengthens the air column below your finger. Because the volume of air above the water in the straw has grown slightly larger without any new air entering the straw, that air now exerts less pressure than the air below the water in the straw. Because the air pressure above the column of water in the straw is less than the air pressure around it, the water stays in the straw pipette. As soon as you remove your finger, air enters the top of the straw. This makes the air pressure above the water the same as the air pressure beneath it. The water's weight then causes it to fall. The same explanation applies to "Two Ways to Prevent a Can from

[FIGURE 12]

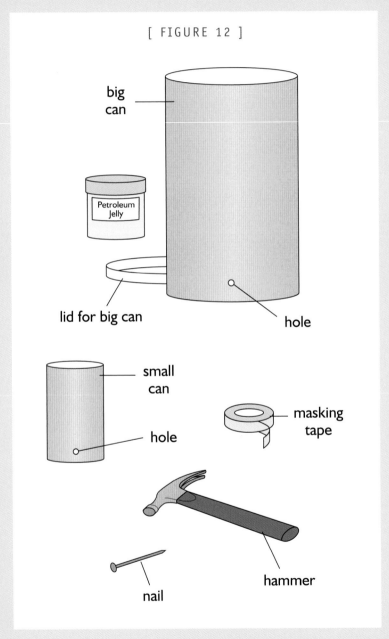

You can make a leakproof can.

Leaking." As water leaks from the covered can, the volume of air trapped above the water increases. This expansion reduces the air pressure in the can. When the sum of the pressures exerted by the air above the liquid and the liquid itself equals the air pressure outside the can, the water stops flowing.

For the opposite reason, you can't drink water through a straw that has a hole above the water level ("A Holey Drinking Straw"). When you drink liquid through a straw, you draw air out of the straw, creating a partial vacuum. The outside air pressure then becomes greater than the pressure in the straw, so water is pushed up the straw. If you make a hole near the top of the straw, air can enter the straw. Since the air pressure in the straw is the same as the air pressure on its outside, there is no force to push water up the straw.

Materials:

- an adult
- medium or large eggs
- 1-liter or 1-quart glass bottle with narrow neck
- cooking pan
- 23-cm (9-in) or larger balloon
- hot tap water
- cold water
- cooking oil
- sheet of paper
- matches
- sink

For this experiment you will need some hard-boiled eggs and a large glass bottle with a mouth slightly smaller than the diameter of a hard-boiled egg. **Ask an adult** to help you boil several eggs in a pan. The eggs should cook in the boiling water for at least 10 minutes.

While the eggs are cooking, pull the mouth of an empty balloon over the mouth of a 1-liter or 1-quart glass bottle. Place the bottle in a pan of hot tap water. What happens to the air in the bottle? How can you tell?

Remove the balloon and let some hot tap water flow into the bottle. Swish the water around inside the bottle so as to warm the air inside. Do this several times. Then put the empty balloon back on the bottle and place the bottle in a pan of cold water. What happens to the balloon as the air inside the bottle cools? What does the balloon's behavior tell you about what happens to air when it cools?

After the eggs have cooked, **ask an adult** to remove the pan from the stove, pour off the hot water, and add cold water. Let the eggs cool in the cold water. When they are cool, remove their shells.

Find an egg that is just slightly larger than the mouth of the bottle. Put a little cooking oil on your finger and rub it around the inside rim

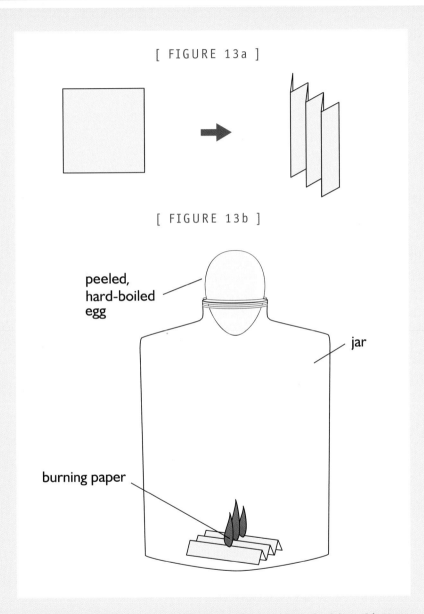

[FIGURE 13a]

[FIGURE 13b]

peeled,
hard-boiled
egg

jar

burning paper

13 a) Fold a quarter sheet of paper in accordion fashion. b) Have an adult light the paper and drop it into a large bottle. Place the hard-boiled, peeled egg on the bottle's mouth and watch.

of the bottle's mouth. This will reduce the friction between the egg and the glass. Next, fold a quarter of a sheet of paper accordion-like, as shown in Figure 13a. **Ask an adult** to light the paper and drop it into the bottle. As soon as the paper enters the bottle, place the hard-boiled egg on the mouth of the bottle (Figure 13b). Why does the egg bob up and down as it rests on the bottle above the burning paper? What happens to the egg when the flame goes out?

What did the burning paper do to the air in the bottle? What happened to the air in the bottle after the flame went out? Why do you think the egg did what it did?

Can you think of a way to get the egg out of the bottle? If not, try this: Fill the bottle with water and turn it upside down over the sink. Put your finger into the neck of the bottle to hold up the egg so that the water and remains of the burned paper can fall into the sink. Next, with the bottle upside down and the egg in its neck, place your mouth next to the mouth of the bottle and blow as hard as you can. When you stop blowing, the egg will fall out of the bottle. Can you explain why?

Chapter 4

Conductivity and the Effects of Temperature on Matter

FOR ELECTRICAL ENERGY TO REACH YOUR HOME, IT MUST TRAVEL THERE FROM A POWER PLANT. Once there, it must be able to be carried (conducted) to all the electrical appliances in your home.

Similarly, to keep your home warm, heat must be conducted from a source to the air in all the rooms of your house or apartment. Since matter provides the "highways" needed to conduct electricity and heat, it is useful to know which kinds of matter are the best conductors, as some types of matter conduct electricity and heat better than others.

In this chapter, you will find out which kinds of matter are good conductors and which are not. You will also discover another way that heat can be transported and how temperature affects the volume of matter.

Materials:

- flashlight batteries (D-cells)
- battery holder(s) or tape and steel paper clips
- insulated wires with alligator clips (if possible) or clothespins or screws
- bulb and bulb holder
- solid objects—nails, silverware, coins, scissors, plastic, glass, wood, cardboard, candles, and chalk
- 6-volt lantern battery
- small plastic or paper cup or vial
- 2 steel paper clips
- water
- antacid tablet (the kind that fizzes)

As you know from experience, an electric lightbulb will not work unless there is a wire leading to and from it that connects to a source of electricity. These wires allow electric charges to flow through the bulb and heat the filament to a temperature high enough to make it glow. The flow of charge constitutes an electric current. The current travels through a conductor. Consequently, metal wires are conductors, but not all solids are conductors. Some solids do not allow charges to move through them. Such solids are called *nonconductors* or *insulators*.

To find out whether a solid is a conductor, you can use the apparatus shown in Figure 14a. One or two flashlight batteries (D-cells) can be placed in a battery holder as shown, or you can improvise your own battery holder by taping a steel paper clip to each pole (end) of a battery.

If you have wires with alligator clips, as shown in Figure 14a, you can clip one end of an insulated wire to each pole of the battery. If you do not have wires with alligator clips, you can use clothespins to clamp the bare ends of the wires to the ends of the battery holder or paper clips. These wires are called lead wires. Clip or screw the other end of one wire to one side of the bulb holder (socket), as shown in the drawing. The wire from the opposite end of the battery can be held firmly against one end of the solid whose conductivity you are testing. A third insulated wire can be used to connect the bulb to the other end of the solid being tested.

You may have to experiment a bit to find the proper number of flashlight batteries and a bulb that lights but does not burn out. Your best bet is to touch the ends of the solid you are testing momentarily with lead wires. If the bulb glows brightly, remove the wires and reduce the number of flashlight batteries. If the bulb glows dimly, you can add batteries or find a more sensitive bulb.

Firmly, but momentarily, touch both ends of the solid you are testing with the ends of the two wires. If the bulb lights, what does it tell you about the object's ability to conduct charge? What do you know if the bulb does not light?

Test a variety of solid objects. You might try various metal objects: nails, silverware, coins, scissors, and so on, as well as solids made of plastic, glass, wood, cardboard, and various other materials such as candles and chalk.

Which of the solids you tested are conductors? Which appear to be nonconductors?

How about gases? Do they conduct electricity? To find out, you will need to use a 6-volt lantern battery in place of the D-cell, because gases tend to be poorer conductors than solids. Slide two steel paper clips over

[FIGURE 14a]

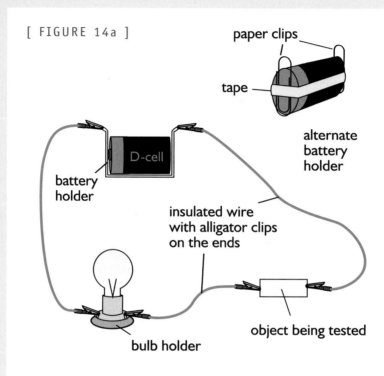

paper clips

tape

alternate
battery
holder

D-cell

battery
holder

insulated wire
with alligator clips
on the ends

object being tested

bulb holder

[FIGURE 14b]

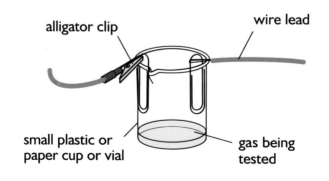

alligator clip

wire lead

small plastic or
paper cup or vial

gas being
tested

14 a) Test solids to see which ones conduct electricity.
  b) A set-up to test gases for conductivity.

the sides of a small plastic or paper cup or vial, as shown in Figure 14b. Connect one lead wire to one paper clip. Touch the other lead wire to the second paper clip. Does current flow when the cup or vial is filled with air?

If the bulb lights, what does this tell you about the gas you are testing?

If the bulb does not light, the gas may be a nonconductor, or it may be a poor conductor.

If air is not a conductor, perhaps carbon dioxide is. You can test the conductivity of carbon dioxide quite easily. Put a small volume of water in the bottom of the cup or vial. The water should not touch the paper clips. Connect the paper clips to the battery and bulb, then add a small piece of an antacid tablet to the water. What happens when the antacid tablet enters the water? What gas is generated? Is carbon dioxide gas a conductor of electricity?

 ## Science Fair Project Ideas

- Which parts of a flashlight bulb are conductors? Is the metal side of the bulb a conductor? How about the small metal knob at the bottom of the bulb? Will the ceramic material around the metal knob conduct electricity? Which parts of a bulb must be connected to a source of electric current if the bulb is to light?
- Carry out an investigation to find out why water to which salt has been added will conduct electricity but water to which sugar has been added will not.
- If gases are not conductors, how does lightning move between clouds or between a cloud and the ground? Do some research to find out how lightning, which is a huge electric current, can move through air.

Materials:

- metal pan
- wooden or plastic cutting board
- freezer
- hot water tap
- wooden bowl
- small metal cooking pan
- glass cooking pan
- large bucket or basin of ice water
- ice
- hot and cold tap water
- 250-ml (8-oz) steel can

- thermometer
- stopwatch, or clock or watch with second hand
- 250-ml (8-oz) glass jar or beaker about as thick as the steel can
- 7-oz Styrofoam cup
- graph paper
- tin can, paper cup, plastic cup, and 2 Styrofoam cups (one with a cover)

(Heat) Conductivity

The ability of a substance to conduct heat is called *thermal conductivity*. The greater the thermal conductivity of a substance, the faster heat flows through it.

Will substances that conduct electricity also conduct heat? To help you answer this question, place a metal pan and a wooden or plastic cutting board in a freezer. Which of these two objects would you expect to be a good conductor of electricity? If you are not sure, how can you find out?

After about 20 minutes, remove the metal and wooden or plastic objects from the freezer. Hold one in each hand. How can you tell which material is the better conductor of heat? Which one conducts heat more readily from your hand?

Let a hot water tap run until the water reaches its maximum temperature. Then fill a wooden bowl, such as a salad bowl, with hot tap water. Immediately thereafter, fill a small metal cooking pan and a glass cooking pan with the hot tap water. From your results in Experiment 4.1, which of the three objects is the best conductor of electricity?

Empty the wooden bowl and turn it over. Place your hand on the dry bottom of the bowl and note how warm it feels. Repeat the procedure for the metal and glass cooking pans. Which of the three solids best conducts heat to your hand?

Substances that conduct heat poorly are called *thermal insulators*. Substances that conduct heat well are called *thermal conductors*. Which of the substances you tested—wood, glass, and metal—would you classify as a conductor? Which would you classify as an insulator?

To investigate conductivity in a more quantitative way, fill a large bucket or basin to a depth of about 5 cm (2 in) with a mixture of ice and cold tap water. Then fill a 250-ml (8-oz) steel can with hot tap water and measure its initial temperature. Put the can of hot water into the ice water and use the thermometer to measure its temperature every minute until it reaches 10°C (50°F). Record the temperatures and times in a table in your science notebook.

Repeat the experiment, using a glass jar with the same amount of hot water at the same initial temperature. Perform the experiment a third time, using a Styrofoam cup.

Plot a graph of temperature versus time for each container. You can plot all three sets of data on the same graph. Examine the three curves on the graph. Which solid is the best conductor of heat? Which is the worst conductor or the best insulator? Would you want to drink hot cocoa from a steel cup? Why or why not?

Put 100 ml of hot tap water into each of five different containers—a tin can, a paper cup, a plastic cup, a Styrofoam cup, and a Styrofoam cup with an insulating cover. Place all five cups side by side and measure the temperature in each cup at 2-minute intervals. Plot temperature versus time for each cup. Plot all the curves on the same graph.

In which cup did the water cool fastest? Slowest? Which material is the best insulator? Does a cover affect the rate at which a liquid cools?

Materials:

- an adult
- ice
- test tube
- metal washer or nut
- clamp to hold test tube
- water
- candle, alcohol burner, or Bunsen burner
- 2 aluminum soda cans
- long, thin stick or wooden spoon
- balance or scale
- graduated cylinder or metric measuring cup
- gloves
- heavy frying pan
- stove
- alcohol thermometer

Liquids are poor conductors of heat. To see that this is true, let a piece of ice slide to the bottom of a test tube. Slowly slide a metal washer or nut down the tube to hold the ice in place. Then add cold water to the test tube. Hold the test tube with a clamp. **Under adult supervision,** heat the water at the upper end of the test tube with a candle, alcohol burner, or Bunsen burner, as shown in Figure 15. You will find that you can make water near the top of the tube boil before the ice melts.

As you might suspect, gases are not good conductors of heat, either. To demonstrate the poor conductivity of air, you can use two aluminum soda cans. If you look at the bottom of a can, you will see that it is not flat.

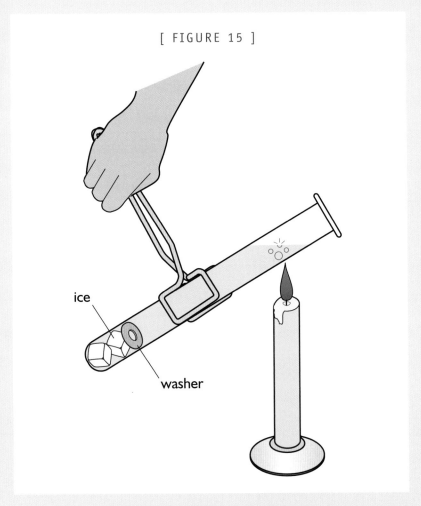

[FIGURE 15]

ice

washer

An experiment shows that a liquid is not a good conductor of heat.

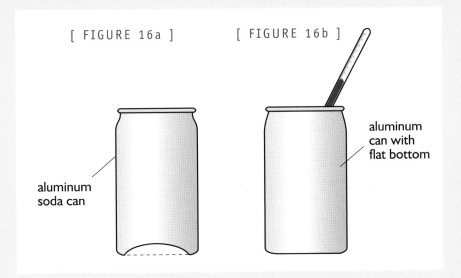

[FIGURE 16a]   [FIGURE 16b]

aluminum soda can

aluminum can with flat bottom

Heat water in two aluminum cans, one with an air pocket beneath it.

Inside the bottom rim it has a domelike surface that provides an air pocket above whatever the can is resting on (see Figure 16a).

Poke a long, thin stick (or the handle of a wooden spoon) into the opening of one of the cans so that it presses against the bottom. Flatten the domelike surface on the bottom of the can by pounding it with the stick or spoon (see Figure 16b).

Pour 100 ml of cold water into each of the two cans. The temperature of the water in the two containers should be the same. Wearing gloves, place both cans in a heavy frying pan. **Under adult supervision,** place the frying pan on a stove's heating element and turn on the heat. Use the thermometer to stir the water in the aluminum cans occasionally. When the temperature of the water in the cans reaches approximately 40°C (105°F), remove both cans from the frying pan, stir the water in both cans, and record the final temperatures. Into which container was more heat conducted? How do you know? How can you account for the difference in conductivity?

Science Fair Project Idea

Make some flat pieces of ice by freezing water in wide shallow plastic dishes or trays. These are some objects that you might place on the surface of the ice: a stack of coins, a marble, a small block of wood, an eraser, a stack of metal washers, a stack of rubber washers, a plastic block, a piece of chalk. Which of those objects, if placed on the ice, do you think will conduct heat from the room to the ice and then sink into the ice? Try it and find out.

Materials:

- large, narrow-necked, rigid plastic or glass bottle (1-liter or larger)
- cold water
- drinking glass
- cloth
- hot water
- balloon
- large (1-liter or larger) glass or rigid plastic bottle
- pan
- refrigerator
- freezer
- test tube
- food coloring
- one-hole rubber stopper
- 15-cm (6-in) length of glass or plastic tubing
- scissors
- thin cardboard
- tape
- pencil or pen
- large plastic containers
- hot tap water
- ice water
- rubbing alcohol

GASES

To see what happens to a gas when it is heated, turn a large, narrow-necked, rigid plastic or glass bottle upside down. Place the mouth of the bottle under the surface of some water in a drinking glass. Warm the rest of the bottle with your hands or with a cloth soaked in hot water. What do you see emerging from the submerged mouth of the bottle? How can you explain what you observe? What happens if you cool the bottle by placing a cloth soaked in cold water on the bottle?

To further examine the effect of temperature on a gas, pull the neck of an empty balloon over the mouth of a large (1-liter or larger) glass or rigid plastic bottle. Put the bottle in a pan of hot water and watch what happens. What evidence do you have that a gas expands when heated?

What do you think will happen if you put the bottle and balloon in a refrigerator for an hour or two? Try it! Were you right?

What do you think will happen if you transfer the bottle and balloon to a freezer for an hour? Do the results confirm your prediction?

What you saw happen to air when it was heated or cooled is true of all gases. If you were to repeat the experiment with carbon dioxide, helium, hydrogen, or any other gas, the results would be the same. Careful experiments show that any gas at 0°C expands or contracts by 1/273 of its volume for each degree Celsius change in temperature. Consequently, the expansion or contraction of a gas with temperature cannot be used to identify the gas.

LIQUIDS

To find out how liquids change when their temperatures rise or fall, fill a test tube to the brim with water to which you have added food coloring. Push a one-hole rubber stopper that holds a 15-cm-long piece of glass or plastic tubing into the mouth of the test tube. The water level should rise about halfway up the narrow tube, as shown in Figure 17.

Using scissors, cut a strip of thin cardboard to fit behind the tube. Tape the cardboard strip to the tube. After 10 minutes, mark the water level on the cardboard, using a pencil or pen.

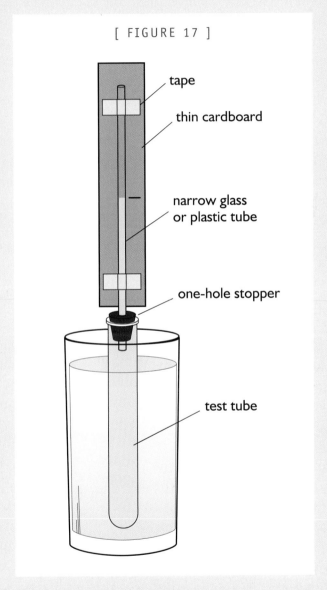

[FIGURE 17]

tape

thin cardboard

narrow glass
or plastic tube

one-hole stopper

test tube

What happens to the volume of a liquid when its temperature rises or falls?

Put the test tube in a container filled with hot tap water. What happens to the water level in the tube?

Mark the final level of the water on the cardboard. Then put the test tube into another container filled with ice water. What happens to the level of the water in the tube? Mark the final water level.

What happens to the volume of the water when the temperature increases? What happens to the volume of the water when the temperature decreases?

Repeat the above experiment with rubbing alcohol in the thin tubing. Does alcohol expand and contract in the same way as water when its temperature changes? Are there any differences in the behavior of these two liquids when they are heated or cooled?

Science Fair Project Idea

To find the *volume coefficient of expansion* for a gas, measure the circumference of an air-filled balloon at room temperature. Record the temperature of the room in degrees Celsius. Record the circumference of the balloon in millimeters. Place the balloon and a thermometer in a refrigerator for about an hour. Then record the temperature in the refrigerator and the circumference of the balloon. How can you use the balloon's circumference to find its radius? Assuming the balloon is spherical, how can you find the volume of the gas in the balloon? How much did the volume of the balloon change per degree change in temperature? By what fraction of its original volume did the volume of air change for each degree change in the temperature?

Materials:

- an adult

- hammer
- two 10-penny nails
- ruler
- 2 wooden blocks, 5 cm × 10 cm × 30 cm (2 in × 4 in × 12 in)
- 2 tables
- C-clamps
- 3-m (10-ft) length of 18-gauge steel wire

- steel washer
- heavy rubber band
- 2 friends
- pencil
- matches
- 4 candles
- 3-m (10-ft) length of 18-gauge aluminum wire (Copper or brass wire may be used in place of the aluminum or steel wire.)

If you have ever let hot running water flow over the screw-on lid of a jar to make it easier to open, you may know how temperature affects solids. Why would the jar be easier to open after it was heated?

You can also do an experiment to see how temperature affects solids. **Ask an adult to help you, because you will be using matches and candles during the experiment.**

To begin, hammer a 10-penny nail into a point near the center of each of two wooden blocks. Then place two tables about 3 m (10 ft) apart. Fasten the blocks to the tables with C-clamps, as shown in Figure 18.

Thread one end of a 3-m (10-ft) length of steel wire through a steel washer and wind the wire around itself several times to fasten it to the

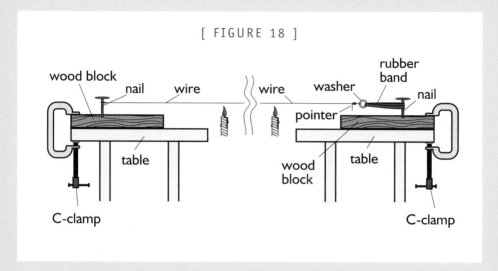

[FIGURE 18]

An experiment shows what happens to the length of a long wire when the wire is heated.

washer. Then thread a rubber band through the washer and loop its two ends over the nail in the first block. Twist the other end of the wire around the nail in the second block. Then pull the tables apart until the wire is almost straight and the rubber band is well stretched.

Bend the end of the wire near the washer so that it points straight down toward the block. Use a pencil to make a mark on the block directly under the end of the wire. Then ask two friends, **under adult supervision,** to slowly move the flames of four lighted candles back and forth along the length of the wire while you watch the wire pointer. Does the length of the long wire change when it gets hotter? How do you know? Mark the new position of the pointer. How much did the length of the wire change?

Repeat the experiment, **under adult supervision,** using aluminum wire. Does the length of the aluminum wire change when it is heated? If it does, how does its change in length compare with that of the steel wire?

Science Fair Project Ideas

- Find out the meaning of *linear coefficient of thermal expansion*. Based on the change in length of the wires and their original lengths, determine your experimental value for the linear coefficient of thermal expansion for the metals you tested, assuming the wires reached a temperature of 150°C.
- How could you revise your experiment to obtain a more accurate value for the linear coefficient of expansion of the metals you tested?
- Investigate some practical applications of the expansion of substances when heated. You might begin with thermometers and thermostats, but there are many more.
- What are some practical precautions that must be taken in the construction industry because materials used in buildings expand or contract with changes in temperature?
- Galileo is believed to have built the world's first thermometer. Find out how he used the expansion and contraction of a gas to measure temperature. Then build a thermometer similar to his. What problems are associated with such a thermometer?

Materials:
- transparent plastic drinking straw
- drinking glass
- water
- food coloring
- clay
- small jar
- marking pen
- freezer
- clock or watch

As you have seen, solids, liquids, and gases contract when cooled and expand when heated. In general, if you cool a liquid to the point where it freezes, it contracts during the freezing process and continues to contract if the solid is cooled further. As a result, the density of the substance increases as its temperature falls, and the solid state is more dense than the liquid state. But water behaves very differently from most other substances.

To see that this is true, place a transparent plastic drinking straw in a glass of water that has been colored with a drop or two of food coloring. Place your finger firmly on the top of the straw, as shown in Figure 19. If you keep your finger on top of the straw, the water will stay in the straw when you lift it out of the glass.

While keeping your finger on the top of the straw, press the bottom of the straw into a lump of clay at the bottom of a small jar. If you remove your finger from the straw now, the water should remain in place.

Once you are sure water is not leaking from the straw, mark the water level in the straw with a marking pen. Put the jar that holds the water-filled straw into a freezer. After about 30 minutes, open the freezer and look at the water level in the straw. Has the water turned to ice? What happened to the volume as the liquid water changed to solid ice? How do you know that the solid ice is less dense than the liquid water from which it came?

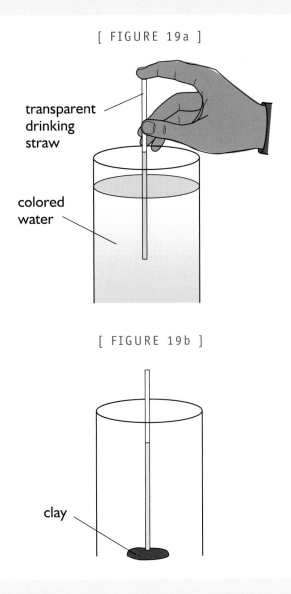

[FIGURE 19a]

transparent drinking straw

colored water

[FIGURE 19b]

clay

19 a) A drinking straw can be used as a pipette to remove water from a container. b) The water can be kept in the straw by using clay to seal off the bottom of the straw. The water can then be transferred to a freezer.

Science Fair Project Ideas

- Investigate the significance of water's abnormal behavior as it changes from a liquid to a solid. What would happen to lake and pond life if water behaved as other substances do when it froze?

- Investigate the meaning of *turnover* as it applies to what takes place in many lakes and ponds during autumn and spring. How is the abnormal behavior of water related to the turnover of lakes and ponds?

- Design an experiment to find the temperature at which water reaches its maximum density of 1.0 g/cm^3. What happens to the density of ice as it cools to temperatures below its freezing point?

Materials:

- an adult
- clear plastic vials
- cold water
- food coloring
- hot water
- eyedropper
- alcohol thermometer
- heated room
- pen or pencil
- notebook
- hammer
- small nail
- small jar with metal lid
- large, clear, tall glass or plastic container

You have found that liquids and gases are not good conductors of heat. But why are water and air used in heating systems? One possible explanation might be that the density of substances such as air and water is related to temperature. Perhaps density differences can be used to transport heat.

To check this idea, nearly fill a clear plastic vial with cold water. Add a drop of food coloring to another vial and fill it with hot water. Now use an eyedropper to remove some of the hot colored water. Next, place the tip of the eyedropper very close to the bottom of the vial of cold water. Very gently squeeze the hot water out into the bottom of the cold water, as shown in Figure 20. What happens? What does this tell you about the density of hot water compared with that of cold water?

Repeat the experiment, but this time nearly fill a clear plastic vial with hot water. Add a drop of food coloring to another vial and fill it with cold water. Very gently squeeze the colored water out into the bottom of the hot water. What happens? What does this tell you about the density

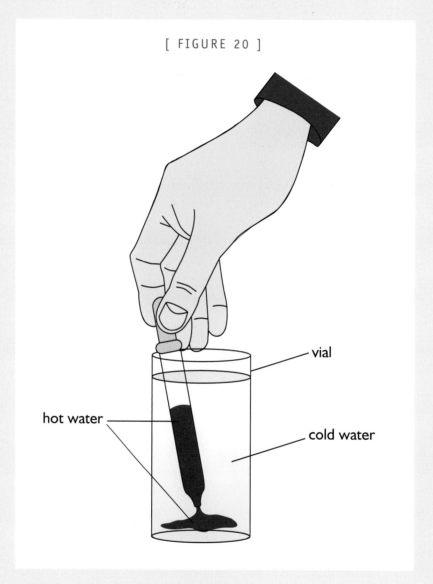

[FIGURE 20]

vial

hot water

cold water

Very gently release some hot colored water onto the bottom of a vial nearly full of clear, cold water.

of cold water compared with hot water? What do you think will happen if you release the cold water near the top of the hot water? Try it! Were you right?

Perhaps temperature affects the density of air and other gases in the same way it affects liquids. To find out, measure the temperature near the floor of a heated room. Be sure the liquid level in the thermometer is not changing before you record the temperature. Then put the thermometer near the ceiling above an inside wall of the same room. After the temperature stops changing, record it. How do the two temperatures compare? What does this tell you?

The movement of fluids resulting from differences in density due to temperature is called *convection*. Convection currents can be found in the ocean and in the atmosphere where they give rise to winds. The wind that you may feel at the beach on a summer afternoon is caused by warm air over the land rising and being replaced by cooler, denser air coming off the water.

To see convection currents on a small scale, **ask an adult** to punch two holes in the lid of a small jar using a hammer and a small nail. A jar such as one in which samples of jelly are sold works well. Next, fill a large, clear, tall glass or plastic container with very cold water. Add a few drops of food coloring to the small jar and then fill it to the brim with very hot water. Screw the lid with the two holes onto the small jar and place it on the bottom of the large container of cold water, as shown in Figure 21.

Watch closely. You will see the colored hot water emerge from the top of the small jar. What happens to this water after it leaves the jar? Try to explain what you observe. Why does the convection you are observing stop after a few minutes?

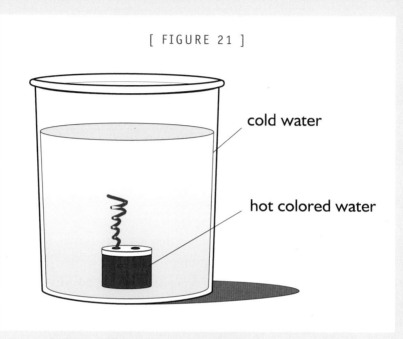

[FIGURE 21]

cold water

hot colored water

An experiment shows convection on a small scale.

 Science Fair Project Ideas

- Investigate the role of convection in the hot-water and hot-air heating systems used to keep buildings warm in the winter.
- What is the significance of 4°C as it relates to the convection of water in lakes and ponds?

Chapter 5

Practical Applications of Chemistry

HOPEFULLY THE EXPERIMENTS IN THIS BOOK HAVE ALLOWED YOU TO BETTER UNDERSTAND THE PROPERTIES OF CHEMICALS AND HOW THEY BEHAVE UNDER CERTAIN CONDITIONS. Perhaps you have gained an appreciation for how chemistry affects you in your daily life. Can you think of any products that you use that were designed by chemists?

A quick look inside the medicine cabinet in your home might reveal a number of medications that are used almost every day by someone in your family. These might include medications prescribed by a doctor to cure an infection, treat an eye irritation, or relieve the symptoms of an allergy. In addition to prescription medicines, you might also find some over-the-counter medications. These can be bought without a prescription and might include pain relievers, stomach-acid neutralizers, and antibiotic creams.

Besides designing medications, chemists also figured out how to make many toiletries such as the soap, toothpaste, and cream that you use every day. Perhaps you or other family members use products such as deodorizers or air fresheners in your home to get rid of smells. In this chapter, you will learn about practical applications of chemistry that range from aspirin to crime scene investigations.

By far the most commonly used over-the-counter medication is aspirin. In fact, aspirin is the most widely used drug in the world. It is estimated that about 1 trillion aspirin tablets have been sold since it was first discovered over 100 years ago. In addition, more than 50 nonprescription drugs contain aspirin as the principal active ingredient.

Most medications are limited to the treatment of one specific problem or ailment. Aspirin, however, is used for a variety of medical problems. Aspirin reduces fever, pain, and the swelling of tissues caused by arthritis. It is also effective in preventing blood clots that can lead to a heart attack. Aspirin reduces the chances of a person developing a repeat episode of kidney stones. No other medication does so much. This is one reason why the aspirin industry has developed into a multibillion-dollar industry since it first began in the late 1800s.

The first recorded use of aspirin actually dates from the early Romans and Greeks. These people discovered that the bark, fruit, and leaves from certain shrubs and trees were helpful in treating pain and other problems. American Indians later discovered that a liquid prepared from the bark of willow trees reduced fever and lessened pain. But these early users of aspirin had no idea about the chemical nature of what they were taking. In the mid-1800s, scientists uncovered the active ingredient in these plants that could relieve pain and do so many other things. This ingredient has the chemical name salicylic acid. Once its chemical identity had been revealed, scientists could make pure salicylic acid in the laboratory.

But the cost of making salicylic acid was high. In addition, the chemical was found to be extremely irritating to the stomach. Then in 1897 a young scientist named Felix Hoffman discovered a way of changing this chemical into something less irritating but still as powerful. What Hoffman made is called acetylsalicylic acid. In 1899 the Bayer Company introduced this new pain reliever to the public under the name aspirin. If you check the ingredient label on a bottle of any aspirin product today, you will see acetylsalicylic acid listed. This experiment will give you an opportunity to analyze an aspirin tablet and see what else it contains besides acetylsalicylic acid.

Materials:
- aspirin tablets
- metric balance
- wax paper
- large spoon or small hammer
- small glass jar
- measuring cup
- water
- sugar test strip (available at a pharmacy)
- Lugol's solution (borrowed from your science teacher)
- eyedropper

Manufacturers list how much acetylsalicylic acid is contained in each aspirin tablet. Check the label on a container of aspirin. Usually, a tablet contains 325 milligrams (mg) of acetylsalicylic acid. But an aspirin tablet contains more than just acetylsalicylic acid. To find out what percent of a tablet is actually acetylsalicylic acid, you must know the weight of a single tablet. Check the label for the weight of a single tablet. If it is not included on the label, weigh several tablets on a balance that measures grams.

Once you know the measurement in grams (g), convert to mg by multiplying by 1,000. Divide the number of mg you get by the number of tablets you placed on the balance. This will give you the weight of a single tablet in mg. A single adult aspirin tablet should weigh about 500 mg. Calculate the percent of acetylsalicylic acid in each tablet by using the following equation:

$$\frac{\text{acetylsalicylic acid (mg)}}{\text{weight of tablet (mg)}} \times 100 = \text{percent of acetylsalicylic acid per tablet}$$

Manufacturers use fillers to give the tablet bulk and to prevent it from crumbling. Both sugars and starches may be used as fillers. To test if your aspirin contains these fillers, fold two tablets in a piece of wax paper. Use a large spoon or small hammer to crush the tablets. Transfer the crushed tablets to a small glass jar and add 1 fluid ounce of water. Aspirin does not dissolve in water, so be sure to swirl the jar gently to disperse the crushed tablet when carrying out the following steps.

Dip a sugar test strip in the liquid. Check the color of the strip against the chart on the container. Does your aspirin contain sugar as a filler? Next, add 10 drops of Lugol's solution to the liquid. A royal blue color indicates the presence of starch. Does your aspirin contain starch as a filler? Finally, calculate the cost per tablet by dividing the price of the bottle of aspirin by the number of tablets in the container. When comparing brands, be sure to compare the price per tablet, not the price per bottle. You can repeat this experiment to evaluate different aspirin brands, including extra-strength products and ones intended for children. Based on your results, is there one aspirin product you would make a point to purchase in the future?

[FIGURE 22]

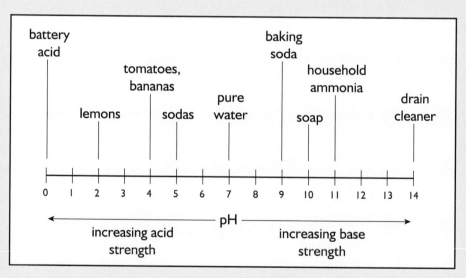

Which of the household items is the most acidic? Which is the most basic?

Science Fair Project Idea

The name *acetylsalicylic acid* tells you something about this chemical. It belongs to a group of chemicals known as acids. An acid can be defined in several ways. One way to classify a chemical as an acid is whether its water solution tastes sour. A more scientific way to classify a chemical as an acid is whether its water solution has a pH of less than 7. The pH of a solution indicates how acidic or basic a solution is and ranges from 0 to 14, as shown in Figure 22. A solution with a pH between 0 and 7 is an acid; one with a pH of 7 is neutral; and one with a pH between 7 and 14 is a base.

The pH of two aspirin tablets in a small glass of water is 2.7. This is about the same as the pH of apple juice. This level of acidity can be upsetting to the stomach of some people. To avoid any problem, these people are advised to drink a lot of water when taking aspirin. This dilutes the acidity of the aspirin. These people can also take buffered aspirin, which is made by combining acetylsalicylic acid with another ingredient. This combination produces a product that has a higher pH value than regular aspirin.

There are several ways to measure pH. You can use a pH meter or pH paper. Check with your science teacher to see if either a pH meter or pH paper is available. You can also measure pH with the help of an indicator. An indicator is a chemical that is used to determine the pH of a solution. Juice extracted from red cabbage is an excellent indicator. Experiment 2.1 describes how to extract and use the juice from red cabbage to see how it is affected by acids and bases. Use one of these methods to check buffered aspirin products to see how much less acidic they are than regular aspirin. Also analyze buffered aspirin as described in Experiment 5.1.

As part of your project, include information on how the buffer reduces stomach irritation. The mechanism involves changing acetylsalicylic acid into something called acetylsalicylate ions. The way buffers work is quite involved. If you decide to undertake this project, check with a chemistry teacher for guidance.

Materials:

- aspirin-substitute tablets (Label must indicate amount of aspirin substitute per tablet.)
- metric balance
- wax paper
- large spoon or small hammer
- 2 large drinking glasses
- measuring cup graduated in mL or graduated cylinder
- water
- small spoon
- clock or watch
- 2 coffee filters
- funnel
- sink

Some people are allergic to aspirin. These people should avoid taking aspirin because they can suffer serious side effects, including stomach bleeding. Those with ulcers must avoid aspirin because it could easily irritate their stomach lining. Children with the flu and a high fever must also not take aspirin because it can cause Reye's syndrome. Reye's syndrome causes severe vomiting and can be fatal. To avoid the possibility of a child developing Reye's syndrome, some doctors recommend that aspirin should never be given to young children, even if they do not have the flu.

To relieve pain and reduce fever, those who are advised to avoid aspirin must rely on aspirin substitutes. Various aspirin-free products are available. One product contains the chemical acetaminophen. Tylenol and Anacin Aspirin Free Maximum Strength Tablets are brand names for products that contain acetaminophen. This chemical does not irritate the stomach or cause bleeding. However, acetaminophen can cause damage to the liver or kidneys if taken in high doses.

Another aspirin substitute is ibuprofen. Advil and Motrin are brand names for products that contain ibuprofen. Like acetaminophen, ibuprofen does not cause Reye's syndrome. But ibuprofen, like aspirin, can irritate the stomach. This irritation can be avoided if ibuprofen is taken with food.

In this experiment, you can analyze an aspirin-substitute product that you may have in the medicine cabinet at home. You can calculate the percent of active ingredient in a tablet using two different methods. One method was described in Experiment 5.1. The following experiment will introduce a second method and also involve percent error. *Percent error* indicates how different the results of an experiment are from the true or actual value. Scientists must consider percent error when reporting a measurement. Here is your chance to do the same.

Scientists use the metric system as discussed in Chapter 1. In this experiment, you will measure only in metric units. You will need a balance that records to tenths of a gram (0.1 g). Check with your science teacher to obtain such a balance. Inform your teacher that you need it to determine how accurate your measurements are. You will also need to measure volume in ml. You may have a measuring cup at home that is graduated in both nonmetric and metric units. If not, ask your science teacher if you may borrow a graduated cylinder like the one shown in Figure 23.

Place 10 aspirin-substitute tablets on a balance. Record their weight to the nearest tenth of a gram. Fold the tablets in a piece of wax paper. Use a large spoon or small

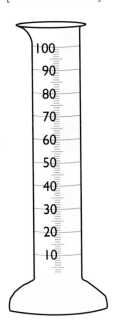

[FIGURE 23]

A graduated cylinder is the most commonly used piece of equipment for measuring volumes in a laboratory.

hammer to crush the tablets into a fine powder. Transfer the powder to a large drinking glass. Add 200 ml of water to the powder. Both acetaminophen and ibuprofen dissolve in water. Use a small spoon to stir for 5 minutes to dissolve as much of the aspirin substitute as possible. Chemicals that are added as fillers do not dissolve in water. By determining how much of a tablet dissolves in water, you can calculate the percentage of the aspirin substitute in a tablet.

Place two coffee filters on a balance. Record their weight to the nearest tenth of a gram. Fold one coffee filter and place it in a funnel. Place the funnel over another large drinking glass. Slowly pour the liquid containing the aspirin-substitute powder through the filter, as shown in Figure 24. Swirl the liquid each time before you pour some into the filter. After all the liquid has passed through the filter, carefully remove the paper from the funnel. Place the filter somewhere where it can dry.

Filter the liquid that you collected in the glass once more. Do this by folding the second coffee filter as you did the first one and placing it in the funnel. Filtering the liquid a second time will trap any solids that may have passed through the first time. This time you can allow the liquid that passes through the filter to empty into a sink. After all the liquid has passed through the second filter, remove the filter and place it next to the first filter to dry.

When both filters are completely dry, weigh them. They should weigh more than before because of the solids they have trapped. Use the following formula to determine the percent of filler in your aspirin-substitute tablet:

$$\frac{\text{weight of 2 filter papers and solids} - \text{weight of 2 filter papers}}{\text{weight of 10 aspirin-substitute tablets}} \times 100 = \text{percent filler}$$

Subtract this value from 100 percent to calculate the percent of aspirin substitute in each tablet. This value represents your *measured value*.

Examine the label on the container of aspirin substitute you used. Note the amount of active ingredient in each tablet. This value is most likely recorded in mg. Multiply this value by 10 to determine the total

[FIGURE 24]

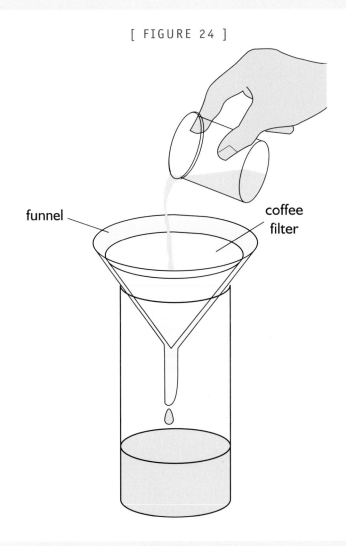

funnel

coffee
filter

Slowly pour the liquid into the coffee filter. Be sure that the level of
the liquid in the filter never gets higher than the top of the funnel.

amount of active ingredient in 10 tablets. Divide by 1,000, or move the decimal three places to the left, to change to g. Use the following formula to determine the percent of active ingredient in each tablet:

$$\frac{\text{total amount of aspirin substitute in 10 tablets (g)}}{\text{weight of 10 aspirin-substitute tablets (g)}} \times 100 = \text{percent active ingredient}$$

This value represents the *true value*.

Use the following formula to determine the percent error in your experiment:

$$\frac{\text{true value} - \text{measured value}}{\text{true value}} \times 100 = \text{percent error}$$

When using this formula, do not be concerned if the difference between the true value and the measured value is a positive or negative value. Disregard the sign and just insert the difference between the two values in the formula.

Do not be concerned if your percent error seems large. There are many possible sources of error in this experiment. For example, some of the fillers used in the tablet may have dissolved in water. How would this affect your percent error? What are other possible sources of error? Can you refine your experiment to eliminate any of these sources?

5.3 Using Distillation to Make Pure Water

Materials:

- an adult
- can of soda
- small cooking pot
- water
- small stones
- aluminum foil
- two clear glass jars of different sizes, with one that can fit into the other
- crushed ice
- large drinking straw
- tape
- stove

A water filter that you can buy in the plumbing section of a hardware store will not remove all of the salts, minerals, and other substances present in water. These filters mainly remove small particles and some of the salts and minerals that make water hard. The salts are present in water as ions. You learned in Chapter 2 that an ion is a charged particle. Ions form when an atom or molecule either loses or gains an electron. As water passes through a demineralizer, some ions are removed. The water that passes through is known as *deionized* water. But even deionized water is not 100 percent pure water, as it still contains some ions in addition to other substances.

To get pure water, you must distill, not deionize. Distilled water is 100 percent pure water and can be made in the laboratory or purchased in a grocery store. The process used to make distilled water is known as *distillation*. If your school has the necessary apparatus, you may have made some distilled water to use when testing pH. But if you have never made any, here is your chance to carry out a distillation using a disposable apparatus. This procedure will not give you enough distilled water to use in an experiment, but at least you will know how it is made.

Open a can of soda and take a drink or empty it until the can is no more than half full. Place the soda can in a small cooking pot. Add some water to the pot, making sure that the soda can does not tip over. You can place some small stones in the can to keep it upright.

Place a smaller glass jar inside a larger one. Surround the smaller jar with crushed ice. Place both jars on a countertop near the stove. Make sure that the level of the pot on the stove is higher than the level of the glass jars on the countertop.

Wrap a sheet of aluminum foil several times around a large drinking straw. Use tape to make sure that the aluminum foil does not unravel when you slide it off the straw. Slide the aluminum tube off the straw. Place one end of the tube into the can so that it rests above the level of the soda. Bend the aluminum tube and place the other end into the smaller glass jar as shown in Figure 25.

Under the supervision of an adult, turn on the burner and gently heat the soda can. Make sure that the pot always contains some water. Observe what collects in the small jar. As the soda boils, some of the vapor makes its way through the aluminum tube. Air surrounding the tube causes the vapor to turn back into a liquid that collects in this small jar. The liquid that collects in the jar is distilled water. If you do not get any distilled water, make sure that not all the vapor formed inside the can escapes into the air. Check for leaks in the aluminum tube. Use foil and tape to seal any leaks. But be sure that you do not completely seal the can or pinch the aluminum tube so that it is constricted. The vapor must not be allowed to build up inside the can where it may cause the can to explode. Taste the distilled water after it has cooled. How does it taste compared with the soda?

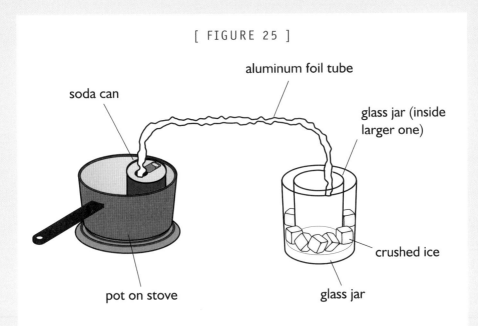

[FIGURE 25]

aluminum foil tube

soda can

glass jar (inside larger one)

crushed ice

pot on stove

glass jar

Water vapor that forms inside the can as the soda is heated is cooled by the air as it travels through the aluminum tube. The liquid then collects in the jar. What might happen if the water vapor stayed trapped inside the soda can?

FRACTIONAL DISTILLATION

A variation of the distillation technique you just performed is known as fractional distillation. *Fractional distillation* is a process that separates the components of a mixture based on their boiling points. This process is used to separate the various components in petroleum—that thick, dark-brown liquid that supplies much of the world's energy. Petroleum is used to make a variety of consumer products, including plastics and many of the top twenty-five chemicals produced in the United States. In turn, these chemicals are used to make other products. Obviously, petroleum is a valuable commodity that contains thousands of different compounds that have become part of our daily lives.

[FIGURE 26]

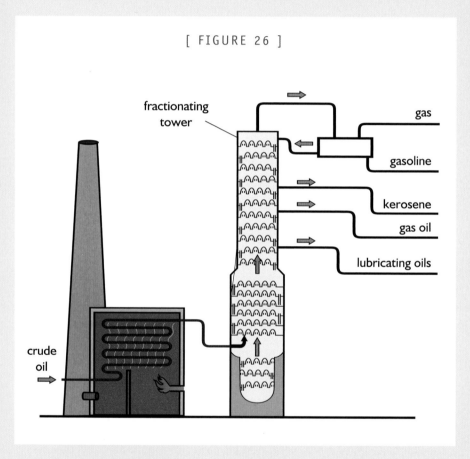

The lightest hydrocarbons with their lower boiling points collect at the top. Which hydrocarbons are these? The heaviest ones with their higher boiling points collect at the bottom. Which ones are these?

All the different compounds in petroleum have one thing in common. They are all hydrocarbons. A hydrocarbon is an organic compound that is made entirely of just two kinds of atoms—carbon and hydrogen. Before petroleum can be made useful, the various hydrocarbons must be separated in the refinery by fractional distillation. This process depends on the differences in the boiling points of the various liquid hydrocarbons present in petroleum. As the petroleum is heated, the liquid with the lowest boiling point vaporizes into a gas first. Cooling this gas causes it to form into a liquid again so that it can be collected and isolated from those hydrocarbons that have not reached their boiling point. As the temperature is increased, hydrocarbons with successively higher boiling points are vaporized, cooled, and collected. Figure 26 shows some of the products that are isolated from petroleum by fractional distillation.

CLOGGED PIPES

The water that comes out of your faucet may be filtered to make it cleaner and softer, but it certainly is not clean and soft when it goes down the drain. In fact, the water may be so full of dirt and grease that it clogs the pipes. Either a wire "snake" or a chemical drain cleaner must be used to unclog the pipe. The snake is simply forced down the drain, pushing out whatever is clogging the pipe. But how does a drain cleaner work? A chemical in the drain cleaner reacts with the grease in the clogged pipe to make soap. The soap can then wash away whatever remains, and the pipe is no longer clogged. Making soap is known as *saponification*. The process of saponification goes back hundreds of years. You can make soap in the next experiment.

Materials:

- an adult
- 2 pairs of safety goggles
- 2 pairs of rubber gloves
- scale
- measuring cup
- measuring spoons
- lard
- granulated drain cleaner (contains lye)
- table salt
- water
- spoon
- rubbing alcohol
- small pot and stove
- large bowl

The early Romans mixed the ashes from burned wood with the fat from sacrificed animals to form a crude soap. In Europe during the Middle Ages, soap was prepared by combining the ashes from burned wood with the fat from goats. With the development of chemistry as a science in the eighteenth century, scientists discovered simpler, cleaner, and cheaper ways to make soap. But all these processes use the same two basic ingredients, as you will find out in this experiment.

Put on safety goggles and rubber gloves and ask an adult to do the same. Ask the adult to mix 454 g (16 oz) of lard with 60 ml (2 oz) of drain cleaner in a pot. Be very careful when adding the drain cleaner because the chemical it contains can cause serious skin burns. If any does spill on your skin or clothes, rinse it off thoroughly in running water. Add 120 ml (4 fluid oz) of rubbing alcohol to the pot.

Ask the adult to gently heat the mixture while stirring. Bring the mixture almost to a boil. Be very careful not to splatter any of the mixture on the stove because alcohol is flammable. Add 60 ml (2 fluid oz) of water and stir thoroughly. While the mixture is cooling, dissolve 14 g (one tablespoon) of table salt in 120 ml (4 fluid oz) of water in a bowl. Pour the cooled mixture of lard and drain cleaner into the salt solution. After allowing the contents to cool completely, remove the solid that forms. This is soap.

The lye in the drain cleaner is a base called sodium hydroxide. You learned in Chapter 2 that a base is a chemical that produces a solution with hydroxide ions. Earlier in this chapter, you read that bases have a pH greater than 7. Sodium hydroxide is a strong base as indicated by the fact that liquid drain cleaners have a pH value of around 14. The sodium hydroxide in the drain cleaner reacts with the fat in the lard to produce soap. You want to make sure that all the sodium hydroxide has reacted so that your soap is not basic, or it will irritate the skin. You can check the pH of the soap you made to make sure that its pH value is less than 8. Refer to Experiment 2.1 for information on how to use an indicator solution to check acids and bases. If the soap is too basic, place it in the pot again and heat it until it liquefies. Continue heating for 15 minutes so that any sodium hydroxide present reacts with the fat. You can also add more lard to the soap.

 Science Fair Project Idea

Lard is only one type of fat to use in making soap. Other animal fats that can be used include goat fat, lanolin, mutton fat, and tallow. Vegetable fats can also be used. These include canola, castor, coconut, corn, olive, palm, peanut, and saf-flower oils. **Under adult supervision**, carry out a project to see what kinds of soaps you can make using these fats and oils. Use a small amount of perfume or aftershave lotion to scent your soaps. Devise some method to evaluate the various soaps you make. You may want to test how well they remove dirt from your skin and clothes.

Materials:

- an adult
- safety goggles
- disposable polyethylene gloves
- animal blood (from packaged meats)
- test fluids: fruit juices, food colorings, theatrical makeup
- absorbent pieces of cotton cloth
- pencil
- paper towels
- 2 eyedroppers or pipettes
- phenolphthalein solution (borrowed from your science teacher)
- hydrogen peroxide solution (3%)

At times, a crime scene investigator will come upon an unidentified dry stain. Is it rust, shoe polish, fruit juice, or dried blood? There is a quick and sensitive chemical test that detects an enzyme (peroxidase) in blood. Peroxidase is found in most plant cells and some animal cells, including blood cells. In blood, this enzyme helps get oxygen to body tissues. Forensic laboratory technicians use the peroxidase test to test for the presence of blood.

Carry out this test under adult supervision. Wear safety goggles and polyethylene gloves. The phenolphthalein solution is flammable; avoid contact with any open flame or hot surface. Do not use human blood.

Have an adult apply drops of nonblood fluids and drops of animal blood from packaged meats to pieces of cotton cloth (such as from a handkerchief). Allow these fluid stains to dry. Use a pencil to number the cloth pieces.

To carry out the test, rub a piece of dry paper towel on the suspected stain. Using an eyedropper, carefully apply drops of phenolphthalein solution to the rubbed area of paper towel. Use a different eyedropper to apply drops of 3 percent hydrogen peroxide over the same area. A positive result for blood is the immediate appearance of a pink color along with some foaming on the rubbed-off trace. The peroxidase test will also provide a strong reaction with traces of blood too small to be seen. A negative result (no pink and no foaming) indicates the complete absence of blood. Can you correctly identify which numbered cloth piece(s) contained bloodstains?

Science Fair Project Ideas

- The peroxidase blood test can produce false positives, meaning that when the test chemicals are added, a pink color along with foaming results even when the fluid is not blood. The reason is that other peroxidases (plant and animal) are present in the suspect stain. For example, a green vegetable smear may produce a positive test result. Learn more about the peroxidase reaction. Visit your school library or learn about peroxidase enzymes on the Internet. Create a data table that records peroxidase test results from various natural substances: fruit juices, tree saps, and other plant fluids that can cause a stain. Apply these substances on pieces of paper towel and allow them to dry. Record which substances show a foaming (positive) reaction following the application of the test solutions. Hint: Investigate what happens if you test a stain created from crushed fresh horseradish root (loaded with peroxidase!) mixed in a tablespoon of red fruit juice.

- Test if warm temperatures and extended time periods (days, weeks) affect peroxidase test results on previously positive test substances. Do positive tests develop more slowly?

FURTHER READING

Books

Baldwin, Carol. *Acids & Bases.* Chicago: Raintree, 2005.

Bochinski, Julianne Blair. *The Complete Workbook for Science Fair Projects.* Hoboken, N.J.: John Wiley and Sons, Inc., 2005.

Lew, Kristi. *Chemical Reactions.* New York: Chelsea House, 2007.

Manning, Phillip. *Atoms, Molecules, and Compounds.* New York: Chelsea House Publishers, 2008.

McMonagle, Derek. *Chemistry: An Illustrated Guide to Science.* New York: Chelsea House Publications, 2006.

Moorman, Thomas. *How to Make Your Science Project Scientific.* Revised Edition. New York: John Wiley & Sons, Inc., 2002.

Solway, Andrew. *From Gunpowder to Laser Chemistry: Discovering Chemical Reactions.* Chicago: Heinemann Library, 2007.

Walker, Denise. *Chemical Reactions.* North Mankato, Minn.: Smart Apple Media, 2008

Internet Addresses

Andrew Rader Studios. *Chem4Kids.* 1997–2008.
http://www.chem4kids.com/index.html

Funburst Media LLC. *Funology: The Science of Having Fun.* 2008.
http://www.funology.com/laboratory/

Try Science/New York Hall of Science. *Try Science.* 1999–2008.
http://tryscience.org/experiments/experiments_home.html

INDEX

A

acetaminophen, 94, 96
acetylsalicylic acid, 90–93
acid-base reactions
    batteries, 12, 15, 40, 43–44
    bleach-stain, 13–14
    concentration, determining,
        36–38
    conductivity, 39–42
    indicators, 29–33, 93, 94
    neutralization, 34–38
    overview, 27–28
acids, properties of, 27, 29–31,
    39, 93
alloys, 16–17
aneroid barometers, 49–53
aspirin, 90–93

B

barometers, 49–53
bases, properties of, 27, 29–31,
    39–40, 93, 105
batteries, 12, 15, 40, 43–44
blood testing, 106–108
brass, 17

C

chemical analysis, 94–98, 106–107
chemistry, 11, 89–90
conductivity, electrical
    acid-base reactions, 39–42
    in gases, 64–67
    in liquids, 39–42
    overview, 63
    testing for, 64–67
conductivity, thermal
    convection, 85–88
    in gases, 71–73
    linear coefficient of thermal
        expansion, 81
    in liquids, 71–73
    solids, 68–70
convection, 85–88
corrosion, 12

D

deionization, 99
density
    convection, 85–88
    defined, 18, 24
    measurement, 24–26
    in thickness determination, 18–20
distillation, 99–103
drain cleaner, 103, 105

E

electrons, 11
experiments, designing, 6–7, 95, 98

F

fillers, 91–92, 96
fractional distillation, 101–103

G

galvanization, 15–20
gases
    conductivity in, 64–67, 71–73
    temperature effects, 75–78, 87
graduated cylinders, 95

H

heat conduction. *See* conductivity,
    thermal.
Hoffman, Felix, 90
hydrocarbons, 101–103

I

ibuprofen, 95, 96
indicators, 29–33, 93, 94
insulators, 64, 69
ions, 27, 30, 39–42, 93, 99

L

linear coefficient of thermal
    expansion, 81
liquids
    chemical analysis, 106–108
    conductivity in, 39–42, 71–73
    temperature effects, 75–78,
        86–87
lye, 105

M

mass, 18
matter, 11
medications, 89–90
mercury barometers, 49–51
metals
    conductivity in, 64–67
    galvanization, 15–20
    redox reactions, 15–17
metric system, 21–23

N

neutrons, 11

O

osmium, 26
ounce to grams conversion, 18
oxidation, 11

P

percent error, 95, 98
peroxidase reaction, 106–108
petroleum, 101, 103
pH, 29–33, 92, 93
pipettes, 55–56, 82–83
pressure
    air, 47, 53, 55–62
    defined, 45
    water depth and, 48–52
protons, 11

R

redox reactions
    bleach-stain, 13–14
    metals, 15–17
    overview, 11–12
reduction, 11
Reye's syndrome, 94, 95

S

safety, 8–9
salicylic acid, 90
saponification, 103
science fairs, 5, 8
scientific method, 6–7

SI units, 22–23
soap making, 104–105
sodium hydroxide, 105
solids
    chemical analysis, 94–98
    conductivity in, 64–70
    temperature effects, 79–80, 87
steel, 17

T

temperature
    convection, 85–88
    defined, 45
    gases and, 75–78, 87
    liquids and, 75–78, 86–87
    measurement of, 46
    solids and, 79–80, 87
    thermal conductivity and, 69–70
thermal conductivity. *See*
    conductivity, thermal.

titanium, 17
titration, 34–38
true values, 98

V

vacuum effects, 55–62
variables, 6–7
volume, 18, 24–26, 95

W

water
    distillation of, 99–103
    pressure, 48–52
    properties of, 82–83
water displacement method, 24–26
water filters, 99

Z

zinc atom radius, 20